FAITH AND
SCIENCE
MATTERS

FAITH AND SCIENCE MATTERS

Series Editor: **Michael O'Hearn**

NOVALIS

Cover design: Blair Turner
Layout: Audrey Wells

Published by Novalis

Publishing Office
10 Lower Spadina Avenue, Suite 400
Toronto, Ontario, Canada
M5V 2Z2

Head Office
4475 Frontenac Street
Montréal, Québec, Canada
H2H 2S2

www.novalis.ca

Library and Archives Canada Cataloguing in Publication

Faith and science matters / edited by Glenn Byer.
(Faith & society series) Includes bibliogaphical references. Issued in print and electronic formats. ISBN 978-2-89646-407-4 (pbk.).--ISBN 978-2-89646-822-5 (epub).-- ISBN 978-2-89646-837-9 (pdf)

1. Catholic Church--Doctrines. 2. Religion and science. I. Byer, Glenn, 1961- ,editor of compilation II. Series: Faith & society series

BX1795.S35F34 2013   261.5'5088282   C2013-902812-9
C2013-902813-7

Printed in Canada.

We acknowledge the financial support of the Government of Canada through the Canada Book Fund for business development activities.

5 4 3 2 1   17   16 15 14 13

Contents

Introduction

THE CHURCH AND SCIENCE: A COMPLICATED AFFAIR

Glenn Byer

Dr. Glenn Byer holds a Master of Arts in Liturgy from Notre Dame and a Doctorate in Sacred Liturgy from the Pontifical Institute of Liturgy in Rome (Sant'Anselmo). A native of Busby, Alberta, he grew up on a farm, where he says, "We always had a great crop of rocks!" His father kept a collection of the most interesting stones that they had picked, and this led Glenn to an ill-fated attempt to become a geologist. His interest in the sciences has stayed with him over the years, and he believes that the natural world is an essential teacher for those who want to seek God with their whole heart. The music of the spheres, the beauty of the mountains, the miracles of molecular biology and the new frontiers of physics, all of this helps to inform a life of faith, to dig ever deeper into the relationship between the creator and the created. Glenn has taught in various colleges and institutes, has helped with the design of churches and has spent the last decade in the business of communicating the Gospel in the printed and electronic word.

Whether in the classroom or the boardroom, or at the kitchen table, for many people the conflict between science and faith seems misplaced. We hear extreme voices on the one hand claim that evolution is an attack against God, while on the other hand there are those who claim that they can copyright human genes. Calls for ending Catholic school systems or installing the Ten Commandments in courthouses all sound like so much posturing. None of this kind of activity will advance either faith or science, since, when we really think about it, all of these approaches are flawed.

Theologians and people of faith should support and embrace the work of scientists as they uncover God's plan in the universe. Scientists and those who seek a strict separation of Church and state should likewise hear the wisdom from people of faith who see a need for limits in scientific investigations of this same plan. And so while the sibling rivalry between faith and science runs deep in public discourse, our efforts in this book belong to a long tradition of a middle way, of faith informing science informing faith.

When we look at the history of the Church, and equally at the history of science, we become more aware of the fact that the image of the priest–scientist runs deep in the Church's tradition. Wikipedia, for all its flaws, lists well over 200 cleric–scientists worthy of an entry in that resource. Throughout the history of the Church there have been people of faith digging deeper and deeper into how the universe works, following wherever the research led. This has at times led to conflict with church leaders.

Maybe this should not come as a surprise, given that there are such similarities in the methodologies of science and theology.

Consider the methodology of faith: from our experience of the world, combined with the revealed word of God and the Tradition of the Church, faith makes claims about the purpose of life, the best way to live, and the natural law that will help life to be lived in as meaningful a way as is possible.

Now the scientific method: from empirical observation of the measurable universe, laws of nature are proposed, tested and retested by peers and revisited by scientists in every generation. New evidence requires new experimentation.

Both faith and science use our interaction with the universe, both in the cosmos but also in our backyards as the primary source of information. Add to that the traditional understandings of that universe, and we can offer theories concerning the fundamental laws of how and why the universe came to be, how it continues to exist and change, and what its ultimate end will be. It is not so different after all.

On a more profound level, it is useful to note that neither faith nor science claims to have invented anything. The laws of nature, the claims about how life came to be, and the vision that they hold on the nature of the universe are understood under the rubric of discernment or discovery. The purpose and workings of the universe are not dependent upon us knowing them. They exist, and regardless of whether we are by faith discerning the meaning and purpose of the universe or by scientific inquiry unlocking what has been unknown in the structures of atoms or galaxies, we are all of us explorers.

And so it is that faith and science should be partners in this journey of discovery. One of the main reasons for having Catholic school systems, and especially for having Catholic colleges and universities, is to advance this partnership.

In chapter one, we consider how, as science extends our vision into the cosmos and so back in time, the canticle of creation becomes a symphony of praise. What does faith discern and contribute to the discussion about cosmic events like the Big Bang? Faith knows that God allows creation to unfold in infinite love, and the wonderful order of the laws of physics have long been seen as proof of this unfolding love.

In chapter two, and much closer to home, as close as the grass under our feet, we reflect on the science of the living world. The evolution of life on earth should not be a threat to faith. As the scientific processes by which evolution happens are uncovered, and as the environmental causes that move evolution forward are enumerated, statements of faith can and should arise. Faith wonders who our neighbour is, and science is showing that what we burn in Canada affects those who live in Australia. Likewise, our neighbours in the evolutionary ladder are now known to be much closer than we once thought. The growing understanding of great apes, dolphins and other animals now places claims on people: they, too, are our neighbours.

Chapter three asks, "What about human beings?" The journey to map genomes, the avalanche of new information about how our brain works, the discovery of cures and the emergence of new diseases, studies on the effects of drugs of all kinds, and new investigations about life in the womb – all of this has raised questions for scientists about the nature of human life. For people of faith, these efforts can be reassuring, in that they more and more show how fragile life can be, and how much in need of protection all life is.

But at the same time, these efforts have occasionally raised immensely difficult moral questions. A commitment in faith to what people of faith have discerned as the culture of life bumps up against what is technically possible. We are better off when faith and science reason together to find a way forward.

And in the end, chapters four and five help us to see that we need to find the best way forward on this blue marble that is the earth. Stewardship or conservation, whatever you call it, shows there is hope for the future of the planet that guides the best of science and religion. While dooms-day prophecies may get the most press, and while some even decry the efforts to preserve the planet as contrary to some sort of apocalyptic will of God, most people of faith and science believe that there are things we can and should do to care for the earth that God has given us.

For its part, government and industry need to ensure that standards are kept that will lead to a sustainable economy within a sustainable environment. Choices have to be made that will lessen the consumption of natural resources and curb the output of the economy. Both faith and science see such restraint as flowing from their reflection and study.

We are publishing *Faith and Science Matters* in response to concerns raised by Catholic teachers of math, English, history, science, business and other subjects who do not feel adequately prepared to deal with where the Church stands on the numerous scientific questions they face in the classroom. So we hope with this book to give you some familiarity of how science and faith cross paths, as it were, in various areas and give you the confidence you need to deal with questions that arise, or, at the very least, to know what the answers are *not*, and maybe where to go for extra information.

A bright future is possible. Faith tells us it is desirable, science assures us that there are ways to make this so. Maybe this book will help teachers and parents and colleagues carry on this conversation in a spirit of mutual respect and of joy in the adventure. The journey of discernment and discovery is far from over!

Chapter 1

FAITH AND THE COSMOS

Br. Guy Consolmagno, S.J.

Br. Guy J. Consolmagno, SJ, is a research astronomer and planetary scientist. He taught physics at the University of Chicago until his assignment to the Vatican Observatory in 1993. The coauthor of five books on astronomy, he is also curator of the Vatican meteorite collection in Castel Gandolfo, one of the largest in the world. His research explores the connections between meteorites and asteroids, and the origin and evolution of small bodies in the solar system. In the year 2000, the International Astronomical Union honoured his work on meteorites and astroids with naming of asteroid 4597 Consolmagno.

How do we come to know God? This question is at the heart of all religious experience and ultimately of all human experience. And it is – and must be – the question behind our scientific experience of the universe.

The role of human understanding

This insight was directly stated by St. Paul in the first chapter of his Letter to the Romans: since the beginning of time, God has revealed himself in the things he has made; namely, in this physical universe. This is illustrated throughout the Bible, our record of the times and ways that God has made himself manifest: from the breath of activity over the chaos described in the opening of Genesis, to the burning bush seen by Moses, to the still, soft voice heard by the prophet Elijah, as described in the First Book of Kings.

If God expresses himself in creation, then our experience of God is mediated through our created human senses; the way our senses experience God's creation is at least one way that we come to know God. This is why we do science. Indeed, "How do we come to know God?" is ultimately the question that shapes the choices we make about what science we do, and the standard against which we judge the success of our work. But science is more than merely experiencing the universe; science is all about understanding what we have experienced. Our reflections about this experience, the way we come to know its meaning, are also mediated through our own mind's processing of what it senses.

In spite of these innate human limitations, we do nonetheless grow in our knowledge of God by experiencing what God reveals in the universe. That this is possible is a tribute to the power of God and the nature of the gifts of understanding that God has given us.

Insight and image

One of those gifts is reason. But even in science, reason does not operate alone, in a vacuum. Science itself also is dependent upon the tools of *insight* and *image*. Insight is what guides us; it directs our hunches about where to look, and it suggests how to apply our reason to understand what we see when we look there. Image allows us to shape our newly won understanding so that we can communicate it both to others and to ourselves, and to remember what we have understood after the flash of insight has passed.

No image is perfect. Indeed, any attempt to treat an image as perfect turns it into an idol. But so long as we recognize an image for what it is, it can allow us to become emotionally familiar with the way we understand God, and thus incorporate our insights into the way we live and interact with God in this physical universe.

What are cosmologies?

When a common image underlies all of our understanding of the universe and how it works, we call that image a *cosmology*. To think about the universe without resorting to some sort of cosmology is impossible.

Our choice of cosmology not only allows us to understand what we see, it also suggests new places to look and the necessity for a new understanding of those things we learn that do not easily fit into our given cosmology. For example, accepting Newton's cosmology with its laws of motion and gravity was necessary before we could notice that the path of Uranus was being slightly perturbed from the orbit predicted from a simple application of Newton's laws; this "perturbation" implied the existence of a previously unseen planet and led to the discovery of Neptune. In the same way, our understanding of Einstein's General Relativity leads us to interpret observations of the motions of galaxies as evidence for the existence of Dark Matter and Dark Energy. Without the predictions of an underlying cosmology and its sense of what is to be expected, we would not recognize that any observed behaviour was "anomalous" – that it differed from our expectations. If you don't have any expectations, you can never be surprised.

But, like any image, our cosmologies are always imperfect and incomplete. If held too tightly, they can turn themselves into idols that get in our way of understanding the reality of nature, or of God.

To take one example, recall that one of the most powerful images we have to help us come to know God is that of "Father." In recent times, as we struggle to understand the role of the sexes in the contemporary setting (where improvements in technology and pressures of population, for example, have altered our expectations about traditional gender roles), we have come to appreciate some of the limitations of this image. In addition, our personal history – the nature of our relationship with our own father – can strongly colour this image in each one of us, in ways that are as different as every family is for every individual. (As Tolstoy famously put it, "Happy families are all alike; every unhappy family is unhappy in its own way.") Thus, those who had a bad relationship with their own father can often have a hard time relating to God as Father.

Now consider the prime attribute given to God the Father in our Creed: "Creator of heaven and earth." In the days when that phrase was devised, just as the word "father" carried a less-charged connotation than it does today, so too the terms "heaven" and "earth" envisioned a cosmology very different from what we currently believe. (And, of course, future developments in understanding our cosmologies will probably move them beyond anything we could imagine today.) Thus, inevitably, just as there is a personal effect in attributing to God characteristics that are particular to our experiences of our own father, there will likewise arise a tension between the ancient cosmology assumed by the authors of the Creed, and what can survive of that image as our picture of the universe changes.

Cosmologies in context

Consider the following selections from the letters of St. Paul. In Paul's first Letter to Timothy (2:5-6) we read: "For there is one God; there is also one mediator between God and humankind, Christ Jesus, himself human, who gave himself a ransom for all – this was attested at the right time." In Paul's Letter to the Ephesians (1:20–2:1) we read: "God put this power to work in Christ when he raised him from the dead and seated him at his right hand in the heavenly places, far above all rule and authority and power and dominion, and above every name that is named, not only in this age but also in the age to come … You were dead through the trespasses and sins in which you once lived, following the course of this world, following the ruler of the power of the air, the spirit that is now at work among those who are disobedient."

And again, we hear from St. Paul, in his Letter to the Colossians (1:15-16): "He is the image of the unseen God, the first-born of all creation; for in him all things in heaven and on earth were created, things visible and invisible, whether thrones or dominions or rulers or powers – all things have been created through him and for him."

Notice the terms used there: Christ as "mediator" opposed to "the ruler of the power of the air" or "thrones or dominions or rulers or powers." What do these strange phrases mean?

Paul was talking about his culture's cosmology. He assumed that his readers were very familiar with these terms, because they reflect the cosmology of his times – a cosmology very different from ours.

Most of us are familiar with the classical geocentric view of the universe, with Earth at the centre and the sun and planets going around it. But even when we say that, we are bringing to that picture our own modern sense of what "Earth" and "sun" and "planets" mean. In our mind, the images of Earth are the ones seen from space, our bright blue dot, and we imagine that the old cosmology somehow envisioned the moon and its craters, or Saturn and its rings, turning about us as if we were the centre of the universe. But, in fact, that is not at all what the classical picture is talking about. Cosmology is more than just how the pieces are arranged; it's about the very nature of the pieces themselves.

Cosmology and religion

Ancient cosmologies started with the observation that the sky appeared to form a dome over a flat disk on which humans lived. Mirroring this view, the first chapter of Genesis describes God creating a "dome" in the midst of the "waters" separating the waters above and below the land on which plants, animals, and people are eventually placed.

Many ancient cultures advanced and developed this picture by postulating a number of different heavens, or layers of heaven, based on the observation of certain objects in the sky that moved among the other stars – the seven "planets" (including the sun and moon), whose names were given, in many languages, to the seven days of the week. They placed each of those dots of light that we see wandering among the stars – the Greek word "planet" means "wanderer" – into its own sphere, its own sky.

I recall once, a few years ago, giving a talk about meteorites to a group of Native Americans in northern Wisconsin. I was trying to explain what a meteorite was by describing it as a rock that has fallen out of the sky, when an older woman in the group stopped me, and asked, "Which sky?" The cosmology she was operating out of was different from mine, but not all that different from the classical view. In one sense, her asking me "which sky?" is comparable to a scientist asking "which planet?" But really it is a very different question, because it has packed within it very different ideas of what those worlds or skies really mean. And these different layers also fed into these cultures' spiritual beliefs.

This ancient cosmology was adapted by Greek and Roman times as the spherical nature of the earth became understood. (That the earth is a sphere can be seen most dramatically in the circular shadow of the earth on the moon during a lunar eclipse.) The Greek philosopher Eudoxos proposed that the stars were in a sphere encircling the earth, and the planets were embedded in crystalline spheres between the earth and this starry orb. By the time of Ptolemy, a cosmology involving epicycles of circles around points themselves travelling in circles around the earth was able to reproduce with remarkable accuracy the observed motions of the sun, moon, and planets.

Such a cosmology was quite different from the one described in Genesis. This did not lead to a crisis comparable to the Galileo affair, however, because most theologians at that time (see, for example, St. Augustine's book *On Genesis*) still saw in this physical cosmology a reflection of the non-physical universe. Even after the adoption of a cosmology based on a spherical earth, a common feature of most cosmologies was the belief that the physical universe mirrored the spiritual realm.

The physical and the spiritual

This belief often involved positing a "chain of creation" in which different levels or aspects of the physical universe were assigned to different elements, different gods, or different ranks of angels. Those different ranks were given names (thrones, dominions) and are what St. Paul was referring to in his letters, cited above. By the Middle Ages, it was assumed that the home of the saints and the biblical firmament was the outer spheres of the universe; below them were the spheres of each planet, moved by angels, and their perfect eternal circular motions stood in contrast to the irregular and finite movements of objects on Earth. Earth stood not at the centre of the universe, but at the bottom of the chain of creation, only one level removed from the Inferno, or Hell, and (unlike the rest of the universe) subject to its own laws of corruption and death.

C. S. Lewis describes this cosmology in his book *The Discarded Image*: "The spheres are moved by the love of God ... Each sphere, or something resident in each sphere, is a conscious and intellectual being, moved by 'intellectual love' of God ... The planetary Intelligences, however, make a very small part of the angelic population which inhabits ... the vast aetherial region between the Moon and the *Primum Mobile* [thrones, dominions, etc.] ... Below the Moon is the [realm] of the arial beings, the daemons."[1] And, in fact, this is only the beginning of the census of all the different kinds of inhabitants of the universe as understood in the medieval cosmology, a complexity that is only faintly echoed in modern fantasies like the *Lord of the Rings* trilogy.

The Latin equivalent for the Greek word *daemon* was *genius*, and various *genii* were each associated with a different planetary intelligence. Each sphere's genii were the source of gifts and abilities bestowed on human beings: one genius might bestow music, another the gift of speech.

The nature and strength of the genius, and thus the gift, for any given person depended on which planet had the strongest influence on that individual. In this way, astrology was given a firm basis in the cosmology. It is interesting to note that, even while the ancient Hebrews roundly condemned the use of astrology to predict future events because it denied the power of God (see, for example, Deuteronomy 4:19, or Isaiah 47:10-14, or the Book of Wisdom, chapters 7 and 13), they nonetheless accepted that it was a natural way to describe how the universe worked. One can find mosaics of zodiacal constellations in ancient synagogues. In fact, the familiar phrase *mazel tov* is actually a shorthand way of saying that "one lives under favourable stars."

This cosmology was, in fact, a beautiful system that not only underlay the physics and astronomy of its day, but also provided the framework for great literature and music. You can't read Chaucer or Dante without knowing the cosmology they assumed, and which they assumed their readers would also know. Again, to quote Lewis, "Few constructions of the imagination seem to me to have combined splendour, sobriety, and coherence in the same degree. It is possible that some readers have long been itching to remind me that it had a serious defect: it was not true."[2]

Where does Jesus fit in?

It had another defect besides being untrue: it also distracted one from knowing God. This was the point being made in St. Paul's letters. Brian Purfield, a British Jesuit writing for *www.thinkingfaith.org,* interprets Paul's letters as a reaction against that cosmology. As Purfield put it,

> People in Ephesus … [and in] nearby Colossae already had a view about this world and their place in it. According to this worldview, the gods were "up

there" beyond the sky and the people were "down here" on earth. Between the gods and themselves were a whole host of intermediaries. Furthermore, if you were to live a happy life "down here," you had to keep all these intermediaries happy as they were in charge of some area of your earthly life.

Paul had received word from Colossae about how the people were adapting Christianity to their culture. When the Gospel is preached to the Colossians they are told that Jesus is their mediator before God – but they already had many mediators before God and life seemed to work very well. They therefore asked the question: "where does Jesus fit into our system?" In other words, they were trying to take the Gospel and super-impose it upon their already-existing worldview.[3]

By the twelfth century, much of this Babylonian, Greek, and Roman cosmology had been lost to the West. It was, however, preserved by Islamic scholars. And there was some crossover. Johannes Scotus Eriugena had an imperfectly translated copy of Plato which he cited in his ninth-century cosmology treatise *On the Divisions of Nature*. And in the late tenth century, a young French scholar, Gerbert d'Aurillac, who grew up near the border with Spain (which was still Islamic), travelled to Barcelona and learned the secrets of the abacus and the armillary sphere (a representation of the celestial globe made from metal rings and hoops showing the equator, the tropics, and other celestial circles, which could be used to predict the positions of celestial objects in the sky). He introduced Arabic numerals to the West; indeed, his mathematical knowledge was so frightening to people that they started rumours he was really a sorcerer. That didn't prevent him from being elected Pope in the year 999, taking the name of Sylvester II.

Finally, with capture of the Spanish city Toledo and its university and library by Christian forces in the mid-twelfth century, the flower of this ancient knowledge was available once again in the West. The translation of these works from Arabic back into Latin, and their dissemination through the newly developed university system, led to the explosion of knowledge we now recognize as the High Middle Ages.

Still, notice a common trait in all these different ways of putting the pieces of the universe together. Up to this point, there is still an unspoken assumption that when you're talking astronomy, you're also talking religion. One tells you how to go to heaven, the other tells you how the heavens go – to quote the famous quip of Cardinal Baroneus, a defender of Galileo – but they are still referring to the same heaven. The physical and the metaphysical had not yet divided.

That division only occurred in the seventeenth century, with Newton and his laws of physics. We all recall the famous story of how an apple's fall led Newton to his insight into gravity. What we forget is the nature of that insight: that the laws describing the fall of the apple are exactly the same as the laws describing the "fall" of the moon as it orbits around the earth.

The idea that things in the heavens operated exactly the same way as things on earth did was a major shift in our understanding of the nature of the universe. No longer would we think of a "translunary sphere" of perfection beyond the moon, to be contrasted with the sin and corruption of Earth. No longer were the heavens to be confounded with Heaven.

The criticism of the old cosmology in the Hebrew injunctions against astrology, and St. Paul's exhortation to look to Jesus rather than daemons as the mediator between God and Man, had been based on the potential evils seen in a system that could possibly challenge the supreme position of God. The criticism in the new cosmology of Newton was more fundamental: rather than saying the old cosmology was potentially evil, it said that the old cosmology was not true.

Newtonianism

Newtonianism did not erupt in perfect form out of Newton's *Principia*. Newton still saw gaps in his understanding of planetary motions, for example, which he thought might necessitate a direct intervention by God. The deists used these gaps as the basis for their belief in God. Over the next two hundred years, however, the developments of mathematics and philosophy in the period self-styled as "The Enlightenment" succeeded in closing these gaps. By 1800, when Napoleon could ask the French mathematician Pierre-Simon Laplace about the role of God in his celestial mechanics, Laplace could accurately reply, "I have no need of that hypothesis." What had started as deism (belief in the existence of God arising from reason instead of revelation) soon became atheism (disbelief in the existence of God).

However, the human temptation to connect an unreflective cosmology with one's metaphysics did not by any means disappear during the Enlightenment. If anything, it was all the more insidious for being far better disguised.

The operating assumption of Enlightenment cosmology was the mechanism of Newton's laws. Given complete knowledge of the state of the universe, where every particle is located and how they are moving at any given moment, and a perfect knowledge of all the forces acting on those particles, then Newton's laws assert that one can in principle calculate perfectly both all the previous states of every particle in the universe and every future state. Obviously, it might be beyond the ability of any human being to make such a calculation; but nature itself was doing the calculations.

This immense deterministic system seemed unshakable. And the only role left for God in such a system is to set the initial conditions, to be (in the Aristotelian sense) the "Prime Mover," the Great Watchmaker who built the watch, wound it up, and set it running on its inexorable course.

What is a "rational" explanation?

Beyond the obvious fallacies of such a system in the light of contemporary physics (according to the Heisenberg Uncertainty Principle, the "exact knowledge" of a particle's position and momentum, for example, is meaningless given the wave nature of matter at the quantum level), there was a more subtle problem with this cosmology. It insisted that every unexplainable experience must have a "rational" explanation, where "rational" was quickly limited in practice to mean the common experience of the one doing the explaining.

G. K. Chesterton, the early twentieth-century British writer who was no fan of Enlightenment rigidity, did not deny the importance of looking for rational explanations.

That was, after all, the plot device of virtually all of his Father Brown mystery stories. (In these stories, the self-effacing priest sees through any number of New Age con men who expect that, because he is a priest, he must be gullibly open to various "supernatural" experiences.) By contrast to the Catholic Chesterton, mystery writer (and creator of the ultra-rational Sherlock Holmes) Arthur Conan Doyle, who was Chesterton's contemporary, was happily deluded by any number of spiritualist frauds in his later life.

And yet, in Chesterton's classic book *Orthodoxy*, he poses the question of whether one should in principle believe in ghosts. The argument of the Enlightenment, after all, was to accept the evidence of one's senses over a blind credulity in received dogma. But what about the testimony in favour of ghosts by those – usually unlettered peasants – who insisted that they had actually experienced them? Chesterton writes, "You reject the peasant's story about the ghost either because the man is a peasant or because the story is a ghost story. That is, you either deny the main principle of democracy, or you affirm the main principle of materialism [the impossibility of ghosts] ... You have a perfect right to do so; but in that case you are the dogmatist."[4]

By being so certain that ghosts cannot exist, one winds up rejecting *a priori* any evidence to the contrary. How is this rational?

The question is not merely academic. It is fair to say that to this day, most people (including the present writer) are extremely skeptical of ghost stories, and yet this Enlightenment attitude also resulted in the rejection of the reality of other natural phenomena that today we must admit are indeed true. My own field of meteoritics is a classic example. Who among us has actually seen a rock fall out of the sky and collected it on the ground? Almost no one ... almost. And yet it does happen, albeit rarely. One such fall occurred in 1803 near L'Aigle, France, a hundred miles west of Paris (and many hundreds of miles from any mountains or rocky outcrops). When the French scientist Jean-Baptiste Biot collected samples of these meteorites from the local peasants and reported on them to scientists back in Paris, many of his colleagues were extremely leery. The American philosopher-president Thomas Jefferson wrote thus about these meteorites to his friend, the surveyor Andrew Ellicott: "The exuberant imagination of a Frenchman ... runs away with his judgment ... It even creates facts for him which never happened ..."[5] But today we have in our collections many pieces of the fall from L'Aigle, and any number of repeatable laboratory tests can convince us that this rock did not form on Earth, and, furthermore, that it spent many millions of years exposed to cosmic rays in space.

Yet Jefferson did have a point. Our experience of the physical world is mediated by our human senses; and our senses can be fooled. Our understanding of what we see is mediated by what we expect to see, which is to say, by our personal cosmology. There is nothing wrong with this. It is a necessary way of dealing with the universe. We cannot use up our time and energy testing every claim on our senses.

As a meteoriticist, I am constantly brought bits of rock by people who think they might have a meteorite. Almost all of them are not – they are what we jokingly call "meteor-wrongs," not meteorites. But in one case, a sample someone brought me really was identifiable as a piece of extraterrestrial rock. So I test every piece, even knowing that the chances of success are rare.

On the other hand, I also hear many tales of UFOs. I give no credence to any of them; life's too short to waste my time on untestable, unverifiable reports. There are, alas, no artifacts from any UFO that we can test in a lab. I am not alone in this skepticism; most astronomers agree with me. (I find it telling that amateur astronomers, those who spend large amounts of their free time outdoors with telescopes and are actually well practised at looking at the sky at all hours under the best of conditions, are among the most skeptical of UFO reports.)

Does this mean that, at some future date, a real extraterrestrial spacecraft might show up and we'll all miss it? That is distinctly possible. The person who does find such evidence of an alien visitor (should it be there to be found) will be someone who has approached the problem with the passion to do so, and an irrational faith that "the truth is out there" waiting to be found. Such irrational belief is, in fact, the hallmark of a fanatic. Such fanatics do on occasion succeed in convincing the rest of us. The vast majority of them, however, wind up wasting their lives on falsehoods that blind them to the truth that actually is out there.

The "Big Bang"

This is the price we pay for our cosmology. But it means that, even today, the separation between what we study in the physical world and what we believe when we begin that study is much closer than most of us would like to admit. The physical and the metaphysical may be separate; but the metaphysical controls the way we choose to understand the physical.

Perhaps the most ironic modern example of how our assumptions about the universe colour the degree to which we are willing to accept the evidence of science is in the history of the idea that the universe is expanding from an initial point in time.

Newton's insight that the falling apple and the orbiting moon obey the same laws of physics has been extrapolated into what is now called the *cosmological principle*: there is no privileged place in the universe. The laws of science are the same everywhere, and at every time. Indeed, this has long been extended to imply that the universe was without bounds in space or time.

Thus, when a Belgian mathematician, Georges Lemaître, suggested in the late 1920s that a universe described by Einstein's Theory of General Relativity might in fact be expanding, his suggestion was treated with great scorn in many quarters. A universe where the space between galaxy clusters was actually growing implied that there must have been a time when that space was much smaller and the total energy density in the universe much higher. Indeed, Lemaître had postulated that one could calculate a specific point in time when the space between all matter was zero and the energy density infinite – a point that could be identified in some way as the "beginning" of the universe.

Speaking for the majority of cosmologists at that time, the English astronomer Fred Hoyle recognized that having such a special time in the universe was a direct violation of the cosmological principle. Even when the American astronomer Edwin Hubble discovered that distant galaxy clusters were in fact visibly moving away from us, in a manner completely in agreement with Lemaître's suggestion, Hoyle responded by inventing an alternative model for the universe (involving the continual creation of space) rather than accept what he sarcastically referred to as Lemaître's "Big Bang" theory.

We know the result, however. The overwhelming evidence from astronomy over the last fifty years has supported the predictions of the Big Bang and ruled out Hoyle's alternative model. We now recognize that, in one sense at least, there was a time (if not a location) that was singular in the history of the cosmos.

God and the physical universe

Why did Hoyle feel so uncomfortable with a universe that had a given starting point? And why didn't Lemaître feel the same unease? It may be that Hoyle, who was not a religious believer, was suspicious of a theory that might be viewed as consistent with the Genesis version of a creation – especially since Lemaître, a scholar with two doctorates (in mathematics and in astrophysics), was also a Catholic priest!

Perhaps Lemaître's religion made him more comfortable considering the possibility of a universe with a beginning point, yet he himself rejected any theological significance to his theory. Lemaître realized that all cosmologies, including his own, are human approximations to a universe much greater and richer than any theory can ever encompass. As such, cosmologies are shaky grounds on which to base one's faith. (It is also worth remembering that, in spite of their scientific and religious disagreements, Hoyle and Lemaître were the best of friends.)

In fact, this is the same message we read in those passages from St. Paul cited at the beginning of this chapter. St. Paul was arguing that his followers should not try to squeeze their religion into their contemporary cosmology. Of course, that was a hopeless request. We can't help but think about the universe except with the terms and the assumptions that make up our own current view of how the world works. Our understanding of life and our place in it is based on the assumptions of what this life is all about – on our own personal cosmology.

Understanding that point, however, leads us to a deeper insight. If a cosmology is our human attempt to come to know the Creator, then we should not be surprised to find that it is forever incomplete. The physical universe is God's way of revealing his infinite self to us. We should never fear what truths we learn about the physical universe. But we should never expect to come to the final word on that topic.

Chapter 2

FAITH AND CREATION

Katharine Stevenson

Katharine Stevenson has been a Catholic educator for over twenty years with experience as an elementary teacher, a secondary religion teacher, a department head, and a Religion curriculum consultant. She is currently a Catholic high school administrator in the Halton Catholic District School Board. Katharine's first love was the biological sciences. She holds an honours Zoology degree from the University of Western Ontario. Part way through her teaching career, Katharine discovered a new love in the area of theology. She returned to academic studies and holds a Master of Religious Education as well as a Master of Arts in Theology from the University of St. Michael's College at the Toronto School of Theology. Her earlier passion for biology was reignited through an emphasis on eco-theology, earning her a certificate of specialization from the Elliott Allen Institute for Theology and Ecology. Katharine now endeavours daily to foster an eco-consciousness in her two young boys so that they might fully appreciate the wonders of God.

Nature is a book whose history, whose evolution, whose "writing" and meaning, we "read" according to the different approaches of the sciences, while all the time presupposing the foundational presence of the author who has wished to reveal himself therein.

Pope Benedict XVI

Justin sat in my Grade 12 religion class with arms crossed defiantly against his chest. The focus of the day's lesson was Christian anthropology. I was recounting the story of creation from the Book of Genesis, focusing particularly on the creation of the first humans and the religious meaning to be gleaned from that account. This teaching is one that is very dear to me. In this scriptural account, we learn that we are created in the image of God, and thus possess an inherent dignity. My students are continually fed messages by the media that they don't quite measure up. Students respond by consuming material goods that promise a better lot in life. Again and again, I attempt to counter these messages by teaching my students that they are fearfully and wonderfully made. They are an image of God on earth. They possess a dignity that, despite what the culture would say, does not need to be earned. They are known and loved by God.

As I taught, my eye was continually drawn to Justin. He was clearly not buying the message. When I had the opportunity, I spoke to him at his desk. He emphatically informed me that he believed in science. He then proceeded to go on to describe what that belief entailed. In the end, Justin concluded that all this talk of the creation of humans by God was nonsense and that no one who believed in science could believe any of these stories. When he finished talking, he stared at me as if to say, "Your move." I smiled and revealed that I had a background in biology and shared his passion for science. I told him that a religious understanding of creation informed by scientific understanding was of great interest to me and that I would really enjoy the opportunity to share my thoughts with him. Justin's face clearly read confusion. He had not gotten the response he had expected – or perhaps that he had experienced in the past when voicing such challenges. I had shown Justin respect by acknowledging his beliefs and inviting him into dialogue. The teaching earlier in the class, that humans possessed inherent dignity, was experienced in that brief exchange, and Justin's posture relaxed. And the dialogue began ...

As an educator in the Catholic school system for the past two decades, I have found Justin's response characteristic of many students who attempt to reconcile our faith tradition with their "modern sensibilities." Take, for example, the two accounts of creation from the Book of Genesis. The first (Gen. 1:1–2:3a) is the systematic account of the origin of all creation over a six-day period, from the emergence of light to that of humans. The second (Gen. 2:4b–3:24) tells the specific story of the first man and woman to be created. Not surprisingly, when these stories are put into conversation with the scientific account of evolution, questions emerge. Did life on earth appear over a series of six days or a span of millions of years? Were there an original man and woman from which we can trace our origin, or did the human species evolve from a wholly other ancestral species? How can religion and science both be correct? Is it possible to accept the scientific theory of evolution and still be a faithful believer? To this final question, a faithful Catholic can respond, yes!

As one who is also an instructor of teachers pursuing additional qualification in religious education, I know that our educators struggle with these same concepts but also desire to enter into dialogue with other "Justins" if given the language to do so. The discussion that follows provides a reflection on a series of foundational issues that must be addressed to support the contemporary Catholic understanding of the creation stories in the Book of Genesis. This Catholic stance toward Sacred Scripture honours the revealed truth of the Bible as well as the truth offered to us through the language of modern science, which includes the theory of evolution.

In this dialogue between these two important ways of knowing, we recognize that biblical stories offer a revelation communicated by God and expressed in human words. These words carry an imprint of the historical period when the revelation was received within a community of faith. The data and propositions of science provide information in the language of the different scientific disciplines, concerning the character of the natural world of which we are a part. In our modern age, both forms of knowledge contribute to the education and development of the whole person. The revealed wisdom of Scripture contributes in a special way to our awareness of the love of God and the salvation history narrative in which we are all invited to participate.

From simplicity to complexity

During my work as an elementary school teacher, I would be invited from time to time to share my insect collection with the Grade 2 students to support their science unit. With each specimen box that I opened, the students would gasp at the variety of insects, all precisely pinned and displayed. Rapid-fire questions would ensue as the students attempted to press their faces as close to the insects as possible. It was a wonderful opportunity to highlight the diversity of this class of arthropods as well as to demonstrate how science clusters living things according to like characteristics (although inevitably, I would then be known as the "Bug Lady" and would regularly be presented with various creatures for my collection by the well-intentioned students).

How has the great diversity of life that we experience on earth come to be? Evidence in the rock layers of Greenland currently suggests that life on Earth existed as early as 3.8 billion years ago. The earliest known organisms are believed to be single-celled bacteria. During the biotic history of our planet, Earth has witnessed at least five mass extinctions and the birth of countless species. The biodiversity on this planet is the result of a complex process known as evolution. All species are descendants of ancestral species that inherited traits that allowed them to survive and reproduce in their particular environment.

Evolution over time occurs by a number of mechanisms. Charles Darwin described the mechanism of natural selection in *The Origin of the Species*, published in 1859 (though written in 1844). The environment is composed of biotic factors (competition from other species, food availability, disease, etc.) and abiotic factors (climate, water sources, soil conditions, etc.). An individual with inherited characteristics better suited to a particular environment will produce more offspring and pass on its genes, and thus favourable traits, to following generations. These traits can contribute to the overall fitness of an individual in the sense that it is able to survive and reproduce. Hence, Darwin used the term "survival of the fittest" to describe those species favoured by natural selection.

Today, the theory of evolution is a widely held scientific theory founded on a large and growing body of evidence that allows scientists to explain observations and make predictions about the natural world. The evidence for evolution includes fossil records, comparative anatomy of homologous features, DNA analysis, and the geographic distribution of living organisms.

The scriptural story of creation: understanding origins

Science continues to seek an ever deeper understanding of the origin of life on earth, and its evolution, using the methodology of science. The world's religions have also sought to understand the origin of life on earth, but for a very different purpose. The creation stories of religious traditions provide a theological or a philosophical under-standing of a creator-god, or of the human person, or of the created world. They are not intended to be scientific accounts. Let us look at one such foundational creation story to develop further this distinction between *evolution* in the scientific sense and *creation* in the religious sense.

The Jewish and Christian Scriptures begin with an account of God's creation of the heavens and the earth (Gen. 1:1–2:4a).[1] The Book of Genesis states that, prior to the first day of creation, when God had created the heavens and the earth, "the earth was a formless void and darkness covered the face of the deep" (Gen. 1:2). This ancient Hebrew concept of a "formless void" invites the reader to imagine an environment without shape or form, while "the deep" suggests that the earth was covered in water. Add the imagery of "darkness," and we have an environment uninhabitable for humans. Then, God begins the systematic work of creation over six days:

1. light (day and night)	4. lights of heaven (sun, moon and stars)
2. sky (separation of upper and lower water)	5. birds and sea creatures from the water
3. a. dry land (earth and seas) b. vegetation	6. a. animals from the earth b. humans (male and female)

Note the narrative structure of the account. The first three days of creation establish the setting for the "creatures" of the next three days. On the seventh day, the Genesis account states that God rested, instituting a holy, "Sabbath" day.

It could appear that the authors of this account were attempting a scientific explanation of creation. The creation over six days seems quite systematic. However, when we take into account the context within which this story was written, a different purpose may be inferred.

This story of creation from Genesis can be classified as a "cosmogony" narrative characteristic of sixth-century BCE Mesopotamian culture. Other well-known creation myths, or cosmogonies, of the time included the *Enuma Elish* and the *Epic of Gilgamesh*. (A *cosmogony* is a story of the origin and development of the universe or the earth, as opposed to a *cosmology*, which considers the structure and changes of the universe. Modern scientific cosmologies make use of the tools of science to study and describe the universe, including its composition and governing laws.) The Genesis creation story is an ancient cosmogony that makes use of a narrative structure to develop ideas about the origin of a world that is completely dependent upon a creator-God. Had the creation account of Genesis been intended as a scientific explanation, the authors might conceivably have described the creation of the sun prior to that of light. Biblical scholars believe that the Book of Genesis underwent its final edit in the sixth century BCE, during a time when the people of Israel were in exile. As such, the narrative is used to highlight themes that would have been important to these exiled people. In the first creation story, these themes include the emphasis on the will of the Creator that all of creation procreate and fill the earth, and on a God who blesses all of creation and finds special favour in humans. Recognizing this style of storytelling, the people of the ancient Near East would have understood this account as a *vehicle* to come to an understanding of God, creation, and the place of the human person within the created order.[2] The intent of this story is to communicate religious truth, not scientific truth.

The Catholic Church acknowledges the narrative function of the creation story of Genesis to reveal religious truths. The *Catechism of the Catholic Church* states, "God himself created the visible world in all its richness, diversity, and order. Scripture presents the work of the Creator symbolically as a succession of six days of divine 'work,' concluded by the 'rest' of the seventh day. On the subject of creation, the sacred text teaches the truths revealed by God for our salvation, permitting us to 'recognize the inner nature, the value, and the ordering of the whole of creation to the praise of God'" (CCC no. 337).

The human person as image of God

Biologists have helped us to understand what makes humans unique as a species. Such attributes include bipedalism, a large brain relative to body size, and hands capable of fine motor skills. Evolutionary biologists continue to piece together the ancestral line in the evolution of the human species. The relationships among ancestral hominids are refined as new fossil evidence emerges. Ongoing scientific research aids in the overall understanding of the human species in relation to, and subject to the same evolutionary processes as, other species.

For an understanding of the human person from a *religious* perspective, adherents of a particular faith tradition look to their sacred scriptures and the interpretation of those scriptures within their faith community. Let us then return to the story of creation in the Book of Genesis to see what religious truth about the human person this scripture story provides.

The creation of humans in the first account of creation in the Book of Genesis occurs on the sixth day. It is perhaps humbling to note that on this day, God also creates animals.

While God finds each day of creation to be "good," only on the sixth day does God declare all creation to be "very good" (Gen. 1:31). Of all God's creatures, it is only to the human creature that God speaks. Only the human is described as possessing this unique intimacy with the creator.

Again, if we consider the historical context of this creation story, we can gain some insight into what it means for humans to be created in the image of God. In ancient Egypt and Mesopotamia, the pharaohs and kings of the time were believed to the representative of god on earth. In the Genesis account, all humans are created in the image of God; therefore, *all* human beings represent God on earth. To be named as God's representative would have inspired great hope among the Jewish people of the time, who were enslaved and in exile. The use of the word "image" is also interesting, considering the Jewish prohibition against fashioning images of God (and hence the law against worshipping idols). This prohibition, however, applies to fixed images. By the freedom of the human person, humans become God's *dynamic* representation.

St. Irenaeus (ca. 130–200 CE) was bishop of Lyons and is a Father of the Church. He was the first major theologian to reflect on the concept of humans being created in the image of God. According to Irenaeus, humans were not created with possession of the full image and likeness of God. That which is created (humans) cannot fully be that which is uncreated (God). Irenaeus reasoned that humans are on a journey of growth toward the perfected image and likeness of God. We are in a process of becoming, as is all of creation. However, this "process of becoming" does not

equate to the scientific process of evolution. We are journeying toward the religious concept of full union with God.

What's your story?

Before moving from this discussion of Scripture to the
Church's understanding of evolution, I would like to raise
one final point. When seeking to explain how God could
have created the world in six days, there are those who,
understanding the purpose behind these creation accounts,
might say, "That is only a story. It is not *really* true." We
need to be careful when we say that the words of Scripture
are stories. The stories of the Bible remain the word of God
presented in human language conditioned by the ages when
these stories became part of the deposit of the community
of faith. As such, the stories offer truths about our relationship with God and God's plan of salvation. We also need to
be clear that the truths offered through Scripture are not
the same in their intent or content as the truths of science.

For some, the struggle can be located in their understanding of the truths offered by the Bible and the truth
provided by science. Others wrestle with the idea that a
story can contain a truth, which in the case of Scripture
has been granted by God to a people of faith. I have taught
some educators who have been uncomfortable with the
use of the word "story" in relation to the Genesis account,
feeling that it devalues Scripture. I usually respond in this
way: When we ask someone, "What's your story?" what we
are really saying is, "Tell me about yourself. Who are you?
What are the experiences that have shaped you into the
person that you are today?" The scriptural story informs
an understanding of who I am. That story, interpreted

again and again in the community of the Church to which I belong, teaches me that I am in relationship with a loving God. It teaches me that I am one part of the goodness of God's creation and that I must serve as God's image on earth by caring for that creation, which God also loves. But this story alone is incomplete. I am not only a human person created in the image of God. I am also a member of the species *Homo sapiens*. The scientific story of evolution is also the shared story of all humans that informs who I understand myself to be. Just as I can teach those students in Grade 2 how the various insects in my collection have developed structures and mechanisms to survive in their particular habitat, so too can I learn how the same evolutionary process has shaped the human species. I have hands that can type on this keyboard. I stand upright and can play hockey with my boys. I have a complex brain capable of reflection on what it means to be human. So, if I were asked, "What's my story?" the narratives of both science *and* my faith tradition would be required to describe my understanding of what has brought me to this moment.

Having now provided an overview of the scriptural account of creation, we will investigate the response of the Catholic Church to modern evolutionary theory.

Evolutionary theory and faith

High school biology textbooks that present the topic of evolution will contain the obligatory section detailing the development of this theory. Often, there is mention that this new theory conflicted with the prevailing religious and philosophical beliefs of the time, which asserted that all creatures were created in their present form. As an educated man, Darwin knew that his ideas would be controversial. It is very appropriate and indeed helpful to students to think about the impact of the new scientific propositions on the religious culture of the time. However, as a Catholic teacher, I recognize that that the textbook presentations of these issues have the potential to plant seeds of doubt in students who are left to wonder if evolution continues to challenge religious beliefs today. As is the case with the philosophical traditions grounding Western thought, the Church has come a long way from its ancient understanding of creation dominated by the idea of its being a one-time act and unchanging. It would be helpful to the general process of education if our high school biology texts could provide a brief overview of how religious understandings of particular concepts have evolved in relationship to the development of scientific theories and discoveries. Such a program would, however, add greatly to the challenge of developing textbooks for students of biology. As such, it falls to teachers to guide the students through these histories.

Let us once again begin this discussion by recalling the foundational distinction between faith and science. Scriptural texts, such as those of Genesis, along with the teachings of the Church, provide a religious interpretation of the sense and the purpose of creation. The Church does not get into the procedural details of evolution. That is more appropriately the role of science. Pope Benedict XVI was very clear regarding the delineation between faith and science, cautioning the religious believer and the scientist to recognize the limits of their discipline. One can no more expect Scripture to explain the laws of evolution than science to prove the existence of God!

However, to suggest that belief in the God of creation excludes belief in the theory of evolution, or vice versa, is "absurd," according to Pope Benedict. Recognizing the need for both faith *and* science, the pope noted that, "on the one hand, there are so many scientific proofs in favour of evolution which appears to be a reality we can see and which enriches our knowledge of life and being as such." But, as he goes on to say, "evolution does not answer every query."[3] The pope invites us to recognize that even when science succeeds marvellously, offering explanations for some of nature's deepest secrets, significant questions will remain for philosophy and theology to address with their particular concerns and methodologies. Scientific questions (e.g., How did the universe come to be?) require scientific endeavour. Philosophy and theology, however, approach their big questions (e.g., What gives meaning to our lives and relationships?) from a completely different perspective. There will be fruitful exchanges between these different fields of inquiry. The concerns and methods of the sciences will, however, remain separate from those of philosophy and theology. The structure of DNA, for example, is hardly the forte of the philosopher or theologian per se. And scientists in their capacity as, say, physicists or astronomers would be uninterested in christological issues, such as how Jesus can be both divine and human. Yet the relationship between the humanity and divinity of Jesus Christ remains a profoundly important issue for Christians. The Pope is stressing that there are questions appropriate to science that are addressed with scientific tools, and there are questions of meaning and purpose appropriate to theology and philosophy that are addressed with theological and philosophical tools. In short, the types of questions being asked determine the most appropriate methodologies for the response.

With respect to the theory of evolution, the Church is generally not opposed. In his 1950 encyclical *Humani Generis*, Pope Pius XII found no immediate opposition between evolution and the doctrine of the faith and did not forbid research and discussions by scientists and theologians with regard to the doctrine of evolution. He called for an open dialogue so that varying opinions on the theory could "be weighed and judged with the necessary seriousness, moderation and measure" (HG, no. 36). In the spirit of dialogue, Pope Pius also noted that such study must also be open to the judgment of the Church, "to whom Christ has given the mission of interpreting authentically the Sacred Scriptures and of defending the dogmas of the faith" (HG, no. 36). Along this line of thinking, the Pope made the following distinction. He stated that the study of the origins of the human body from pre-existent and living matter would be study appropriate to the sciences, as it deals with an understanding of the material world. However, any questions concerning the human soul would not be appropriate to the scientific endeavour, since such questions move to the realm of the supernatural. Pope Pius articulated the position of the Church in this matter, stating, "the faith obliges us to hold that souls are immediately created by God" (HG, no. 36).

In 1996, Pope John Paul II wished to update the Church on its position relative to the theory of evolution. He acknowledged that, almost a half-century after *Humani Generis*, "new knowledge has led to the recognition of the theory of evolution as more than a hypothesis" that has been widely accepted by researchers in various fields.[4] Pope Pius XII had found no opposition to the theory of evolution and the teachings of the Church. This is support of the theory, but in a rather passive way. John Paul II was much more direct in the credibility the Church ascribed to the theory of evolution. The weight of evidence from several scientific disciplines allowed the Church to state confidently that the theory of evolution is more than mere hypothesis. It is indeed the best scientific explanation of the origin of life on earth that we have.

Pope Benedict XVI was very supportive of ongoing dialogue between scientists and theologians on the topic of evolution. In 2008, the Vatican hosted a conference sponsored by the Pontifical Academy of Sciences with the theme "Scientific Insights into the Evolution of the Universe and of Life."[5] It is interesting that, given the preceding discussion of the scriptural story and scientific story, Pope Benedict employed similar imagery. In his opening address to the Academy, Pope Benedict noted that "to 'evolve' literally means 'to unroll a scroll,' that is, to read a book."[6] The pope recognized that when considering the ultimate origins of life, "questions concerning the relationship between science's reading of the world and the reading offered by Christian Revelation naturally arise."[7] He went on to reiterate the position of his predecessors, Pope Pius XII and Pope John Paul II, "that there is no opposition between faith's understanding of creation and the evidence of the empirical sciences."[8]

So, we have three leaders of the Catholic Church essentially saying the same thing: the scientific theory of evolution does not stand in opposition to the religious understanding of creation. This seems pretty straightforward! However, the Church has felt compelled to voice some caveats with respect to such sweeping statements of acceptance. One such caveat has already been noted, with respect to the creation of the human soul. In what follows, we will outline the Church's response to various evolutionary "theories," meaning the various explanations used to describe the mechanism of evolution as well as the philosophies underlying the theory. In the spirit of open dialogue, the Church needs to evaluate critically the science in light of its own teachings. The Church has a long-held doctrine of creation, and "theologians have the responsibility to locate modern scientific understanding within a Christian vision of the created universe."[9]

First, the Church teaches that the human person is both body and spirit, or soul. The Catechism states that "every spiritual soul is created immediately by God – it is not 'produced' by the parents – and also that it is immortal" (CCC, no. 366). Therefore, the Church accepts the evolution of the human body from pre-existent matter, but not of the human soul. As we have already seen, this was noted by Pope Pius XII in *Humani Generis*, and has been reiterated by church leadership since. Any theories of evolution suggesting that the human spirit emerges from the forces of living matter are, however, "incompatible with the truth about man. Nor are they able to ground the dignity of the human person."[10] Moreover, one could even argue that any theories of evolution that suggest that the human spirit, understood in a religious sense, emerges from the forces of living matter are incompatible with the scientific pursuit!

This conversation on the subject of the "soul" or "spirit" can, itself, be a little challenging. I think that it is helpful when speaking from a position of faith to understand these as theological concepts. If we equate the soul or spirit with the mind, then we can find ourselves on less stable ground. For example, an article in *The New York Times* states, "as evolutionary biologists and cognitive neuroscientists peer ever deeper into the brain, they are discovering more and more genes, brain structures and other physical correlates to feelings like empathy, disgust and joy. That is, they are discovering physical bases for the feelings from which moral sense emerges – not just in people but in other animals as well."[11] Just as we make the distinction between faith/creation and science/evolution, I think that the same distinction between faith/soul and science/mind could be helpful to this conversation. The *Times* article concludes with a quote from Dr. Kenneth R. Miller, author of *Finding Darwin's God* (1999). This Roman Catholic scientist frequently speaks at college campuses. When asked by the students, "What do you say as a scientist about the soul?" he always responds, "As a scientist, I have nothing to say about the soul. It is not a scientific idea."[12]

Second, the Church teaches that "God needs no pre-existent thing or any help in order to create … God creates freely 'out of nothing'" (CCC, no. 296). No other being has the ability to "create" in this sense, without prior matter. The Church declares that *at the beginning* of the creation of the universe, God was there. This is a statement of faith. The religious truth revealed in the scriptural stories of creation affirms that the universe begins from God as an outpouring of God's love and goodness. The Church does not speculate what was *before* creation. Scripture affirms that God was present "in the beginning." We must not interpret beyond this. The Church does not profess the Creator to be a "God-of-the-gaps" who is used to explain phenomena currently beyond our scientific knowledge. The Church leaves to science the study of *how* the universe first began. With respect to creation from nothing (*creatio ex nihilo*), as paragraph 296 from the Catechism states, theologians find that the Big Bang theory does not contradict this church teaching.

Finally, the Church teaches that "God does not abandon his creation to themselves. He not only gives them being and existence, but also, and at every moment, upholds and sustains them in being, enables them to act and brings them to their final end" (CCC, no. 301). The Church, however, rejects those philosophies, linked by some to theories of biological evolution, which contend that every detail of the universe is predetermined and brought about by the Creator, as some proponents of the Intelligent Design theory claim. In actuality, Intelligent Design theories are varieties of religious "evolutionism" and not science. Intelligent Design theorists use God, not science, to explain the order we see in the universe. They ignore the calls for caution raised by Pope Benedict XVI and others who encourage religious believers and scientists to recognize the limits of their discipline. So how does the Church speak of God's continuing relationship with creation? Rather than determining every detail, God wills all of creation into existence and then allows each creature to unfold according to its own nature. "The universe was created 'in a state of journeying' (*in statu viae*) toward an ultimate perfection yet to be attained, to which God has destined it" (CCC, no. 302). This destination is not in the sense of an ordered, preplanned, physical design for the universe, but in the sense of full *communion* with the Creator. Such statements about God and creation say nothing about evolution and everything about relationship. Out of love, God is present to creation. God guides, nurtures, and beckons creation, but never coerces. God creates a universe that creates itself. I liken this to a loving parent who nurtures the children and sets them on a path of goodness while recognizing that the children must be given the freedom to make their own way. The loving parent walks with the children on this journey.

The dialogue continues

In his 2003 address to the Pontifical Academy of Sciences, Pope John Paul II spoke of his conviction that scientific truth participates in divine Truth and, as such, can help theology and philosophy to understand more fully the human person and God's Revelation, which is "completed and perfected in Jesus Christ." "For this important mutual enrichment in the search for the truth and the benefit of mankind, I am, with the whole Church, profoundly grateful."[13]

His words speak to an understanding of "dialogue" as reciprocal conversation and ongoing communication, the purpose of which is not to reach some conclusion. Blessed Mother Teresa of Calcutta was quoted as saying, "What I can do, you cannot. What you can do, I cannot. But together we can do something beautiful for God." I believe that, as a person of faith, I have much to learn from the wisdom of science if I am open to being transformed by what it has to teach. As humans search for answers to the origins of life, we are enriched by both scientific and religious truth. We need both. Faith and science are not adversaries. The Church will continue to put new scientific knowledge and insights in conversation with religious beliefs in order to deepen a religious understanding of the human person within creation. And the dialogue continues…

Chapter 3

FAITH AND HUMAN LIFE

Moira McQueen

Moira McQueen graduated in law from the University of Glasgow, Scotland, and worked as a lawyer for several years, specializing in family law and juvenile court. After her Master of Divinity Degree from the Faculty of Theology, University of St. Michael's College and the Toronto School of Theology, she earned a PhD in moral theology, also from St. Michael's. She has been teaching moral theology at the Faculty of Theology since 1994, and has written and co-authored several articles in bioethics and other areas and her book *Bioethics Matters: A Guide for Concerned Catholics* was published by Novalis in 2008. Moira was appointed Director of the Canadian Catholic Bioethics Institute in July, 2004.

M any of the bioethical challenges to people of faith today involve the use of technology. These challenges come into play in an important way at all stages and, perhaps especially, at both the beginning and end of life. At the beginning of life, for example, developments in reproductive technologies have brought about changes in the way some people think about having children. For instance, couples who are infertile or who have had problems becoming pregnant can now sometimes have the baby they long for through the process of in vitro fertilization.

Developments in medical science have made this possible. They have also raised ethical issues that the Church has reflected upon carefully. The gift of a child and its inherent dignity are so highly valued that the Church has spoken out strongly against using such technology as a way of bringing a baby into the world. We will consider why this is so later in the chapter.

At the other end of life, when it looks as if people are near death, questions can arise about whether to continue the use of respirators, ventilators, or artificial nutrition and hydration. It may have to be decided if these technological means of supporting life are still benefitting the patient, perhaps because the illness has become terminal and the patient's bodily functions are clearly deteriorating, or because their use is actually causing other medical problems, or distress. These are questions about "futility of treatment" and "burdensomeness."

Can our Catholic faith help us to deal with these questions about the beginning and end of life? The answer is yes. The Catholic tradition has a long-established anthropological approach that provides a helpful context for our moral decision making about these life-and-death matters.

What is anthropology?

Anthropology is the study of the nature of the human person as an individual and in society. There is a developmental aspect to anthropology, observable in different societies over time. Social scientists look for patterns of similarities and differences among cultures. Differences are usually due to varying environments and circumstances, while similarities likely stem from constant features, such as innate human drives towards personal growth, sexual appetite and procreation, raising a family, work, spirituality, and so forth.

Is there a specifically Catholic anthropology? Here we move into the realm of faith and belief as it interacts with social science. For Catholics, this means reflecting on the spiritual aspect of human nature, as well as on the biological, physical, social, and cultural aspects of that nature. First and foremost, the Catholic approach centres on faith in Jesus Christ and on following his way. That "way" is based on his teaching and example, on the teaching and witness of his immediate followers and disciples, on Scripture, and on the development and explanation of our Catholic tradition.

Scripture and anthropology

We find a host of examples in Scripture about the kind of people Christians should be, and how we are to live in the world, exemplified by the "great commandment" given to us by Christ, to love God and to love our neighbour as ourselves. This may sound simple, but doing so consistently can be extremely difficult for most of us. At times, even knowing what "love" entails can be difficult. Nevertheless, embracing the commandment to love is essential to the Christian life and conscience, since it recognizes a radical equality of each person that goes far beyond the provisions of any human laws or juridical rights.

Following Christ also means we are to die to sin. We are to struggle against sin because it rejects God's will and always harms our neighbour in some way, and ultimately harms us. If we steal, cheat, and lie, or if we are violent, negligent, slanderous, or destructive, we clearly harm our neighbour, and in so doing or being we also contribute to shaping values – our own and those of others – in harmful ways.

Christians are called to be the Body of Christ. This means that we must value the person of every member of this Body as our own. Scripture demands a distinctive way of being and behaving in the world that recognizes "the widow, the orphan, the sick, the poor, the downtrodden" as equal members of the one Body. Scripture speaks to our heads and our hearts: parables such as the Good Samaritan and the Prodigal Son can enlighten and inspire us by presenting gospel values that are fundamental to the Christian way of living. When we take these values to heart, they become part and parcel of our makeup, or our anthropology.

The Catholic tradition and anthropology

The Catholic tradition, as expressed in the Church's teaching, reinforces these scriptural aspects. A document from the Second Vatican Council, *Gaudium et Spes,* tells us that our growth and maturity as human beings, and our search for meaning and truth, are inseparably linked to the mystery of God, who is our ultimate goal: "The Church truly knows that only God, whom she serves, meets the deepest longings of the human heart, which is never fully satisfied by what this world has to offer" (GS, no. 41).

A Catholic anthropology acknowledging God is, therefore, inevitably also theological, since only God, who created us in his image, can reveal the "most adequate answers" to our deepest questions about the meaning of life and death, "and this he does through what he has revealed in Christ." Christ was born, lived, and died for us. Through his resurrection he redeemed us from our sins and leads us to the Father. He made us holy, and "the whole of nature created by God" for our use, as well (GS, no. 41). In short, we are created in God's image and redeemed from our sins by Christ's dying and rising. In following Christ's way to the Father, we become the best we can be. Human dignity is firmly anchored and safeguarded in this saving action of Christ. His Gospel proclaims our freedom as children of God and "has a sacred reverence for the dignity of conscience and its freedom of choice" and "constantly advises that all human talents be employed in God's service" and the service of others (GS, no. 41).

To those for whom the transcendent dimensions of these words ring true, reliance on other theories of human nature alone is unsatisfactory. Among other things, "transcendent" means being in a state of realizing and acknowledging the gift of our relationship with God through our relationship with Christ, and wanting to deepen that spiritual relationship by being open to the ongoing revelation of his Gospel, and by following his way in our daily life with others.

Science, including social science, can and does add immensely to our knowledge of the human, but it cannot address questions about the transcendent dimension of morality, values, spirituality, and meaning. Eminent scientists such as Francis Collins, a leading geneticist, director of the Human Genome Project and former atheist, openly recognize that there are matters and events that cannot be explained by observation and rational deduction alone. Collins is very clear about what science can do. And he is equally clear on what it cannot do: "The meaning of human existence, the reality of God, the possibility of an afterlife, and many other spiritual questions lie outside the reach of the scientific method."[1]

Who am I? Why am I the way I am? What is my purpose here? Why do I think the way I do? Why is life so mysterious and, despite our best efforts, ultimately uncontrollable? These questions continue to challenge us as individuals, as groups, as whole societies. They are continually recurring, "ultimate" questions with which every thinking human being has to wrestle. Since these are "why" questions having to do with meaning and purpose, they are ultimately theological in nature.

Similar Christian anthropologies

Since they are universal, such questions are naturally also considered in depth by other denominations. For example, the Faith and Witness Commission of the World Council of Churches issued a document entitled *Christian Perspectives on Theological Anthropology*. It draws attention to a verse from Psalm 8 that contains *the* question: "What are human beings that you are mindful of them, mortals that you care for them?" (Psalm 8:4). There is no easy answer to this question. We live in a complex world, and this precludes any neat and tidy answer. But there is one thing we can assert: human beings are imbued "with something of the sacred mystery which comes from the Spirit or breath of the infinite Creator." This specifically Christian understanding of the human person is deep, not because it is based on some complex, abstract theory of human nature, but because it rests firmly on "truths grasped by faith in the midst of life, suffering and joy."[2]

This aspect of mystery, experienced at the birth of a new baby, the death of a loved one, or the display of human acts of kindness and care, is something to which nearly everyone can relate. Some experiences cannot be captured or fully explained in words, although many of the psalms do capture our longing for this experience. The psalmist says this beautifully: "As the deer longs for running streams, so my soul thirsts for you, my God" (Psalm 42:1). These transcendent experiences can both intrigue and inspire us as we continue the human search for meaning and purpose in life.

A Presbyterian minister, Charles Cameron, suggests that the anthropological question – understanding ourselves – raises the question of God: "Can human experience be adequately understood without reference to God?"[3] Cameron describes secular anthropology as looking at the human person "horizontally," whereas when God is in the picture, we look at the person "vertically" as well. This results in a more complex view of the person, but one that takes spiritual and religious experiences fully into account. In fact, God must be included in the study of anthropology. Cameron disagrees entirely with those who argue that God is a human creation and therefore has no place in anthropology. As people of faith, we believe that humanity is created in the image of God. Theological anthropology says that God is already there and that its task is to direct our attention to the God of hope, especially today, in a world where signs of hope are often few and far between.[4]

The theological anthropology of John Paul II

In his encyclical *Redemptor hominis* (1979), Pope John Paul II shared the same anthropology as the Second Vatican Council. He stressed the centrality of God's love: without it we cannot find meaning and purpose in life. Indeed, we cannot live without it (RH, no. 10). Fortunately, this love has been revealed to us in Christ. This revelation tells us who we are – a redeemed humanity sustained by God's love for us (RH, no. 8).

In considering the relationship of humans and technology, John Paul says that rational and honest planning is required when it comes to the use of the earth's resources. But humanistic planning is also essential; otherwise, nature, and our relationship to it, is threatened. The earth's natural environment is not just there for immediate and selfish consumption. To the contrary, God wants humanity to relate to nature "as an intelligent and noble 'master' and 'guardian', and not as a heedless 'exploiter' and 'destroyer'" (RH, no. 15).

This language of exploitation and destruction may appear strong, but when we consider John Paul's remarks here concerning our natural environment, and later in this chapter consider the question of embryonic experimentation and destruction, it is clearly appropriate. John Paul argues that the development of technology and a more technologized civilization must be accompanied by an equally strong development of morals and ethics. The development of technology, he says, can doubtless improve life for all. But the real question is whether this progress makes us better as human beings. Does this progress make us more mature spiritually and more aware of our dignity as human beings? Does it make us "more responsible, more open to others, especially the neediest and the weakest, and readier to give and to aid all"? (RH, no. 15).

Many Christian thinkers, in line with this approach to humanity, point out that current moral dilemmas created by the development of biotechnologies and genetic engineering involve anthropological questions. Today, numerous anthropologies exist, and this can leave us struggling to assert any one fundamental position. Ultimately, though, they are incomplete because they ignore the transcendent. A Catholic anthropology, on the other hand, strives to capture the fullest picture possible; it considers body *and* soul, and it looks to revelation as well as to the various sciences to help answer our ultimate human questions.

Connections: anthropology, ethics, and technology

Some ethical issues involving technology at the beginning of life

Now that we have looked at some aspects of an anthropology that serves as the basis for a Catholic approach to life in all its dimensions, we may ask how it is employed in light of today's scientific advances. We recognize that, while such an anthropology cannot be completely empirical or evidence based, it must take those approaches into account along with the more transcendent dimensions of our human nature. In that frame of reference, we can look at two contemporary ethical challenges: in vitro fertilization and stem cell experimentation.

In vitro fertilization

It is a sad fact that a significant number of couples who wish to become parents are unable to do so. In North America, approximately one in five couples is infertile, or has serious difficulty in achieving pregnancy. Many turn to the process of in vitro fertilization (IVF).

In this process, the woman's egg and the man's sperm (their gametes) are placed in a laboratory petri dish. A small electrical current is introduced to help the gametes fuse, and, should the procedure succeed, fertilization takes place. This means that a new human being comes into existence, which immediately begins the process of development through various cell divisions and stages until, at around fourteen days old, it must be either transferred to the mother's womb, cryopreserved (frozen), or discarded.

From the perspective of Catholic teaching, IVF is morally wrong in itself because it violates the inseparability of the unitive and procreative dimensions of the marriage act. The long-standing Catholic position is that the act of genital intercourse is of enormous importance both to the relationship of the couple (the unitive aspect) and to the child who may be conceived and born as a result of it (the procreative aspect). When new reproductive technologies came into being, the Church studied their implications and concluded that they do not fully respect either the dignity of the marital act or the dignity of the child so conceived.

For IVF, the woman's ova, or eggs, have to be surgically retrieved from her ovary. First she must undergo a process of hyperstimulation of the ovary to produce more than the one egg that most women produce each cycle. This is because it would be dangerous and counterproductive to surgically remove the one available egg every cycle. The hyperstimulating drugs that are administered are powerful and have their own known side effects. Women must consider the whole process carefully to give informed consent, since the treatment involves drugs and surgery. The man's sperm is obtained through masturbation, and no further action is usually involved, though sometimes he may also receive drug treatments to help improve his sperm count.

In this type of technological fertilization, there is no sexually unitive act. The gametes are obtained separately and are fused by a technician in a laboratory. This treatment of human gametes is far removed from what the Church believes is necessary to ensure the dignified and personal coming-into-being of an individual. In early 1987, the Congregation for the Doctrine of the Faith issued an instruction known as *Donum Vitae (The Gift of Life)*. This document set out the Catholic Church's position on the respect due human life in its origin and on the dignity of procreation. The core of the instruction is this: "The moral relevance of the link between the meanings of the conjugal act and between the goods of marriage, as well as the unity of the human being and the dignity of his origin, demand that the procreation of a human person be brought about as the fruit of the conjugal act specific to the love between spouses" (DV, B 4 c). Conception as the product of a medical or biological technique such as IVF does not meet this criterion.

Many Catholic couples find this difficult to understand, since they are using IVF in an attempt to bring a new life into the world: i.e., they are trying to be procreative. The Church insists, however, that the procreative and the unitive values are each so important that they must be in operation together in every act of sexual intercourse, and this is the case whether couples are trying to achieve or prevent pregnancy. Pope John Paul II reminded us that the unitive and procreative dimensions are integral components of Christian marriage – of marriage in the Lord. They are the essence of self-giving and openness to life. There is always a human tendency to substitute our plans for those of the Creator, and perhaps to put our own needs and desires first, even before those of the child we hope to bring into the world. In vitro fertilization's separation of the unitive and procreative dimensions of the sexual act requires a third-party intervention in the creative aspect and eliminates the unitive aspect. It also exposes the newly created human life to decisions by its parents and others about its very existence, since not every embryo will be selected for transfer to the womb. This is far from the view that every child is a gift from God, whose very existence is life enriching for its parents, and who has been brought into the world through their sexually expressed love. Part of the difficulty in understanding church teaching in this area perhaps lies with our failure to value children as much as we should. Many couples think of children as burdensome and life limiting. Such notions make it difficult to see them as a "gift" from God. Many couples plan their families with a specific limit in mind, and through the technology of contraception, separate the unitive and procreative dimensions of the sexual act to achieve their goal. The reverse side of the coin, when couples cannot have children in the usual way, leaves them feeling deprived of an important part of life. The desire to have children often leads them to turn to methods, such as IVF, that similarly separate the unitive and procreative dimensions of the sexual act.

Church teaching looks to the original design of the Creator and asks us to see that neither type of intervention is consistent with openness to life as God's gift. This is doubtless a difficult question for us, given the widespread acceptance of these medical-technical interventions to promote or prevent the conception of children in our society. But has this acceptance come about with too little reflection on some of the consequences for society and the individual?

Just think, for example, of other ethical concerns with IVF. When a woman undergoes IVF, her embryos are usually tested for genetic and other defects before any are transferred to her womb. Embryos not transferred are usually frozen, but defective ones are discarded. No matter how desperate a woman may be to have a child, she is unlikely to want an embryo transferred to her womb that is thought to be physically or mentally defective, or even potentially defective. It is not too strong a conclusion to say that a form of eugenics is practised in these areas, since only "the best" embryos are selected as worthy of survival.

The Catholic stance is that embryos are human beings, and must be treated as every other person (DV, I 1), that is, with respect for their inherent dignity and right to life. Freezing or destroying embryos clearly does not respect their human dignity.

Stem cell experimentation

Some "unwanted" or "unused" embryos are donated to science for experimentation. In Catholic teaching, anything that disrespects the embryo's life is morally wrong. Stem cell experimentation is one further instance of that disrespect, in that the embryo is viewed merely as an object to be used for experimentation instead of as a human subject already in existence.

For some time now, medical science has looked upon these embryos as golden research opportunities, which allow researchers to probe them for insights into extracting stem cells, for observation of embryonic growth, or for use in developing ways of regenerating tissue and organs.

So-called spare embryos die when used for experimentation. Current law has decided that, although acknowledged as human, these embryos may be subjected to experimentation: their parents consider them as surplus to need, and their fate otherwise is to be cryopreserved or destroyed. Their destruction is seen as secondary to their usefulness in providing information that could lead to medical discoveries. This fosters a utilitarian approach to human life, one that is further intensified when some take the position that, since these embryos are going to die anyway, why not use them?

Catholic teaching, on the other hand, treats human beings as persons (the philosophical or legal term for human beings) from conception to natural death. This terminology is important because only "persons" can be the subjects of legal rights in most jurisdictions. Under Canadian law, embryos, while acknowledged as human, are not classed as persons, and therefore have no legal rights, either to life or to meaningful protection.

Canadian law states that human beings in the embryonic and fetal stages are not persons until they have been completely delivered from the birth canal of their mother, or, as we usually say, "are born." This claim leaves babies vulnerable to being considered non-persons, even when they are in the process of moving through the birth canal, under the current interpretation of the law.

These differing views of the embryo and fetus are, in fact, opposing views of the human being/person. They are opposing anthropologies: the one makes moral decisions on the basis of the belief that what comes into existence at conception is a human being who is to be treated as a person; the other rejects mere existence as bestowing moral status, and relies on criteria that deny human status until the law declares it. The Catholic Church continues to protest against this practice, but society remains divided on the moral and legal status of these smallest of human beings.

Technology has been available for some time to test babies at different stages of fetal life. Both ultrasound and amniocentesis can reveal actual or possible "imperfections," on the basis of which many women choose to terminate their pregnancy. Again we can conclude that the practice of eugenics is steadily increasing in this field as in the embryonic field, as more genetic tests are developed, including those for gender.

Some further consequences of reproductive technologies

Quite apart from the use of embryos left over as a consequence of in vitro fertilization, there are some serious ethical concerns of a social nature. These include third-party gamete (ova and sperm) donors, the sale of gametes in some countries, donor anonymity, the use of surrogate mothers in North America and in less developed countries, and so on.

Third party donors

Some problems of infertility occur because the man's sperm capacity or in the woman's egg production is defective. When IVF using their own gametes fails, some couples turn to gamete donors for help in achieving pregnancy. A woman can be assisted in conceiving through use of another man's sperm. The baby will be the wife's biological child, but not the husband's. In other instances, the husband's sperm may be used with a donated egg. The wife carries the baby to term, but it will not be her biological child. Sometimes a woman cannot carry a baby to term, and she and her husband may turn to a surrogate mother to perform that task for them. Some homosexual couples use donated ova or sperm, perhaps fertilized by the opposite partner to the donor. If males form the couple, they will have to ask a surrogate to carry the resulting embryo to term for them. There are clearly many different scenarios, but a crucial consequence for the eventual newborn is that he or she will be either the biological child of only one of the parents, or, if both egg and sperm are obtained from third parties, the biological child of neither.

The question of identity is extremely important for all of us. Young people born through the use of third party donors may never find out who their biological parents are. In Canada, the sale of gametes is illegal, although individuals can donate them. Donors remain anonymous for reasons of confidentiality, and although children born through IVF increasingly want to know their biological mother or father, that information is seldom available. More and more people born through IVF are challenging the anonymity afforded donors. Discovering their identity, their heritage, their racial and cultural background is essential to them. They want to know what makes them who they are.

The use of surrogate mothers raises questions of both ethics and social justice. Payment for surrogates is not allowed in Canada, although reasonable costs may be met. We can surmise that few women will volunteer to have a baby for someone else at no cost. A nine-month gestation period and several months of restricted activity, followed by labour and delivery, is a labour of love for a natural mother, but why would a surrogate go through that process and then hand over the child to someone else? Motherhood is a gift and a task of a sort, but it was never intended to be only a "task," far less a contract. Some human activities are priceless.

Surrogate mothers may be hired in some countries, including the United States. In some socially disadvantaged countries, surrogates are routinely exploited. The women there are paid far less than in, say, the United States; they are housed away from their families so that their health can be monitored, not for their own sake, but for the sake of the baby; if a miscarriage occurs, the contract abruptly terminates; it is uncertain what happens if a baby is born with some defect, but the tendency is to blame the surrogate. These women are often coerced into signing contracts because of extreme family need. Full consent is so clearly absent that the word "contract" should not even be used. This is a classic example of the commodification of people – these women are being used for someone else's benefit, giving up all claim to their own lives for the time period involved, while risking their own health and safety for the sake of a "customer" whose desire to have a child involves this immoral approach.

These are just a few of the ethical dilemmas associated with the use of reproductive technologies. Other practices, such as selective reduction, gender selection, and the possibility of cloning human beings, among others, raise a whole host of moral and ethical issues. But the examples discussed above show that the Catholic Church's reservations about these technologies have strong foundations. IVF may seem to help individuals, but it is not necessarily beneficial for the common good of society, including, often, the children who are born through that process.

Some ethical issues involving technology at the end of life

At the other end of life, when people may be dying or living with life-threatening illnesses or injuries, the use of technological aids such as ventilators and respirators has resulted in different ethical dilemmas, this time concerning whether or when to begin or end some courses of treatment. While technology can keep people alive so that an initial diagnosis may be made, questions can arise as to its continuing usefulness when it becomes clear that the person cannot be cured of a serious illness, such as a rapidly progressing cancer, or if the patient finds the use of a particular machine too burdensome. It is not always easy to decide which treatments are futile, that is, when it becomes clear that they cannot cure an illness or ensure even minimal recovery of health. At a certain stage, it seems that their continued use simply keeps the person alive in a greatly reduced state.

Catholic teaching allows competent patients or their decision makers to determine whether to continue or to end what is known as "extraordinary" or "disproportionate" treatment when no further curative treatment is possible. This part of the decision-making process involves objective factors, such as the medical facts and assessments of the person's health, and statistical probabilities of the likely success of a particular course of treatment, taking into consideration the person's age, stage, and condition. These factors are called "objective" because they can be assessed, measured, observed, and weighed by health-care teams and family members, although there is an art to this, based on experience, that augments the factual foundation.

The Church also looks to subjective factors, such as the patient's personal experience of burdensomeness in undergoing some treatments, such as being kept alive by technological means. Only the patient can truly determine how he or she is reacting emotionally and psychologically to some treatments, but family and caregivers can often also observe a patient's obvious dislike of some treatments, and can also relate to the patient's distress or suffering. For example, some patients with dementia frequently pull out their feeding tube, perhaps indicating their repulsion at the treatment, or their possible discomfort. In making decisions about discontinuing any treatment, the patient or his or her decision makers must look to both objective and subjective factors, placing them in the broader context of prayer and discernment, as they strive to follow God's will.

If the patient is completely unconscious, it is then impossible to declare the treatment burdensome, since the patient is not capable, as far as anyone can tell, of experiencing either benefit or burden. At this point, a certain circularity defines the theological and bioethical debate about when to end a treatment. This is why we should all reflect on some of these scenarios beforehand, so that we have some idea of what we would want by way of treatment, should a certain type of circumstance arise. Catholic teaching on ordinary/proportionate and extraordinary/disproportionate means is of great value in helping us make these difficult decisions.

Final points

While technology will often provide new choices and opportunities, these new choices frequently give rise to questions that some find difficult to reconcile with our faith beliefs about the meaning and purpose of life and about the decisions we must make in difficult circumstances. The hard work of thinking about these problems must be done individually *and* with the help and guidance on faith and morals available to us as members of the Catholic community. Membership in the Body of Christ reminds us that we are not only to look at how these decisions may affect us as individuals, but we must also consider the wider context of the common good. To return to the IVF issue, for example, couples often say that their decision to use IVF is a private, conscious decision that is theirs alone to make. True, they must make the final decision on the matter, but they should also think about wider social implications. They will most often be asked if they want prenatal genetic diagnosis for their embryos, with obvious implications should any embryo be found to be "defective." Perhaps they will have several embryos made, and will then have to decide what to do with the "spares." They should remember that some of their decisions could reinforce the existing societal tendency to regard the fate of the embryo as irrelevant. For so many people, these "spare" embryos are not regarded as persons, but only as objects available to be used in experimentation for other people's benefit.

Ethical questions for us

We can ask, what would *we* decide in these matters? What do *we* think about the process and implications of IVF? What do *we* think about the status of the embryo? Should society approve of experimentation on spare embryos, since they will be discarded otherwise? Is a utilitarian approach to human life justified in these circumstances? At the end of life, should we able to simply make up our own minds about the use of technology without reflecting on Catholic teaching about objective or subjective factors, or without consideration of the impact our decisions may have on others?

We discussed the existence of different anthropologies at the beginning of the chapter. We saw that Christians believe that we are made in God's image. Church teaching strives to keep us pointed in that direction, and urges us to resist any technology that risks not recognizing the dignity of every human being from conception until natural death. Every human being shares the radical equality of being made in God's image, and no human being, no matter how young or old, is expendable. Any technology that can enhance human life without harming any other person's life is to be welcomed; any technology that harms human life is to be avoided.

It may appear to some that the Church is extremely strict, even negative, in these matters. In reality, it is insisting to one and all that every human life be treated with the respect it deserves, and that no person has the right to decide on another person's continuing existence. God is not selective as to who comes into being. Consequently, neither should we be.

It is, then, the task of the Church to persuade people of the values at stake in our decisions about the use of new technological and scientific advances. Catholic principles are meant to help us deal with the most important questions about life and death. They are meant to help us follow the Way of faith, hope, and charity that Christ embodied. Technology and medical science are to be welcomed in so many ways, but a Catholic approach acknowledges the priority of the flourishing of each individual and of the common good over any technological possibility.

Chapter 4

FAITH AND THE EARTH: PART I

Fr. John McCarthy, S.J.

Fr. John McCarthy, SJ, is the assistant pastor and chaplain of St. Mark's Parish on the campus of the University of British Columbia. Father John is a specialist in boreal forest ecology and the biology of lichens, important biological indicators of environmental conditions. He has conducted extensive studies on the ecology of old growth forests in northern Newfoundland. He served for years as the Co-Chair of the Wilderness and Ecological Reserves Advisory Council for the government of Newfoundland and Labrador. His work in boreal forest conservation earned him the Canadian Environment Award, Gold Prize, from the Royal Geographical Society of Canada.

We live on a human-dominated planet. Earlier generations could never have imagined that so many facets of nature would, one day, come under human control. This control is not exercised by any one nation, culture, or race; rather, this control is multi-dimensional, multi-faceted, and hard to pin down. It is not necessarily a planned regulation of nature. Our control of nature is, rather, largely opportunistic, driven according to the perceived needs of our present age. But one thing is certain – we will decide the future of the planet. We will decide which species and habitats we value, which will be protected and which will flourish or fade. Despite the power we are able to exert over different ecosystems on our planet, we recognize that not all is under our control. The forces of nature are great and complex. We are often unable to predict the consequences of our actions. Along with the great power in our hands in this present age comes the great responsibility to use it wisely.

In this chapter I will examine the discourse between the voices of our Christian communities and the environmental challenges of our age. My analysis will proceed in three stages. First, I will review the current "state of the planet" within the context of what has come to be termed the "Anthropocene." Secondly, I will consider a Christian theological response to this unprecedented challenge. Finally, I will discuss how faith and science are challenged, for the good of all, to act as essential partners in our response to the current ecocrisis.

The Anthropocene: A human-dominated planet

Geologists divide the 4.6-billion-year history of Earth into defined time spans called eons, eras, periods, and epochs. Each division is marked by a well-defined geological or paleontological event. We currently live in the Holocene Epoch, the past 10,000 years since the end of the last glacial period, which has witnessed the rise of human civilization. It seems that we are moving beyond the Holocene into a new epoch.

Human impact on the global environment is now recognized as being so pervasive that some have suggested we are living in the Anthropocene Epoch.[1] The geological community has not formally accepted the term, but the debate has begun. Advocates of the Anthropocene concept claim that we have passed a new juncture in earth history. Humans have altered the earth to such an extent, they say, that the biological and chemical signals of this change will be discernible thousands of years from now. In other words, they claim that we have passed from the Holocene to the Anthropocene, or the Age of Humanity. Proponents mark the year 1800, well into the early years of the Industrial Revolution, as a reasonable beginning to the Anthropocene.[2]

Our human impact on climate change has received much attention recently. The concept of the Anthropocene is being proposed to indicate a new level of awareness that human activity appears to be causing a massive transformation of the terrestrial biosphere.[3]

Humans have been transforming the earth for millennia. Our use of stone tools (ca 2.5 million years ago) and fire (700,000 to 1.5 million years ago) enabled us to transform the environment out of all proportion to our population size. Indeed, our early ancestors may have caused the extinction of megafauna.[4] But it was the development of agriculture that set the stage for our rapid expansion across the planet and for the rise in human culture. The Neolithic clearing of land and the domestication of plants and animals created novel human agrosystems that permitted the human population to increase from several million to billions today. The rise of the Industrial Revolution in the early 1800s marked an unprecedented shift as we learned to use fossil fuel energy, synthesize industrial nitrogen fertilizer, and engineer the world to suit our needs. Our capacity to venture into space and to the depths of our oceans, together with our ability to manipulate the genetic characteristics of life itself, rank among the latest manifestations of our control over the forces of nature and the fundamentals of life.

In 1700, nearly half of the ice-free terrestrial biosphere was wild, without human settlements or substantial land use. Most of the remainder was in a semi-natural state (45%), having only minor use for agriculture and settlements. By 2000, the opposite was true, with the majority (55%) of the biosphere in agricultural and settled anthropogenic biomes, that is, cities, towns, and villages; less than 20% semi-natural; and only a quarter left wild. We passed the 50% mark from mostly wild to mostly anthropogenic, or human-impacted, early in the 20th century.[5] Most of "nature" is now embedded within a heavily modified human environment. So pervasive is our transformation of biomes – those naturally occurring areas, or communities, of plant and animal life that have adapted to the particular conditions of the area – that we have invented the new terminology of "anthromes" to describe biomes heavily modified by human activity.[6]

The Anthropocene: Living beyond our means?

Does this ecological degradation and loss of biodiversity resulting from human activity reduce the provision of ecosystem services (such as food, water, fuel, and recreational values, among others) essential for human well-being? The answer today seems to be yes.

The Millennium Ecosystem Assessment noted that "human activity is putting such strain on the natural functions of the Earth that the ability of the planet's ecosystems to sustain future generations can no longer be taken for granted."[7] Furthermore, "the provision of food, fresh water, energy and materials to a growing population has come at a considerable cost to the complex systems of plants, animals, and biological processes that make the planet habitable."[8] The drivers of this change are multiple and complex; they are demographic, economic, socio-political, scientific/ technological, cultural, and religious in nature. We turn now to look more closely at some demographic drivers.

Beginning in the early nineteenth century, human population began to increase significantly – from less than a billion then to over 7 billion today. It took from the beginning of time to until about 1927 to put the first 2 billion people on the planet; less than 50 years to add the next 2 billion people (by 1974); and just 25 years to add the next 2 billion (by 1999).[9] Global populations are expected to grow to 9.3 billion in 2050 and 10.1 billion in 2100.[10]

The growing human population, which is increasingly urbanized in technology-rich megacities and demanding more and more food, fibre, water, and energy, is placing unprecedented pressure on the planet's natural ecosystems.

Raw population numbers, however, do not tell the whole story. These numbers must be considered together with consumption (and waste) patterns, as well as issues of social justice that determine the flow and distribution of these patterns. It is one thing to note the increasing world population; it is quite another to note that 20% of the world's population consumes 57% of the gross world product and produces 46% of global greenhouse gas emissions.[11] Indeed, the high consumption patterns of North America, western Europe, and Japan exert an impact equal to that exerted by the high population densities of India and China.

Attempts are being made to develop methods that provide a relative measure of this growing human impact. One helpful measure is termed the "ecological footprint."[12] The ecological footprint is an accounting framework that tracks humanity's competing demands on the biosphere by comparing human demand against the regenerative capacity of the planet to meet those demands. In other words, it quantifies the relationship between human consumption of resources and Earth's capacity to continue to provide the resources on which we depend. It does this by assessing the biologically productive land and marine area required to produce the resources a population consumes and to absorb the corresponding waste. The consumption of resources is converted to a normalized measure of land area called "global hectares" and is expressed on a per capita basis.

The strength of the concept of the ecological footprint is its ability to quantify and track over time the relative human consumption and bioregeneration patterns and to detect national and regional changes. The ecological footprint metric provides a way to measure and compare the ability of nations or resource sectors to act sustainably. It is a measure of the impact we humans are having on the earth.

To date, all indicators reveal that given the current rates of resource consumption and waste production (in this case, carbon dioxide [CO_2] only), we are living well beyond our means.[13] Humanity's ecological footprint has doubled since 1966, and in the early 1970s our consumption patterns and waste production exceeded Earth's biocapacity. That trend has continued upward to where in 2008 (using the latest available data), our footprint exceeded Earth's biocapacity (the area of land and productive oceans actually available to produce renewable resources and absorb CO_2 emissions) by 50%. In other words, it would take 1.5 years for Earth to regenerate the renewable resources that we used in 2008 and absorb the CO_2 released by our activity.[14] Whether you call it "ecological overshoot" or "eating into your capital," the message is the same: according to all indicators, we are currently living well beyond our means and risking the development of environmental trends that are likely to impose severe penalties on the ecosystems required for human life.

The Anthropocene: A Christian faith response

Even the power associated with the tools of science and the forces of politics and economics will alone be inadequate to meet the challenges posed by ecological degradation.

While essential, the perspectives provided by the tools of science and social organization will be insufficient to respond to the challenge of forging a sustainable future. We need a higher viewpoint, a public discourse that engages our highest human values and motivations, a discourse that includes the language of respect, care, and love. Such a discourse will, by necessity, consider the religious, sacred, spiritual, and affective significance of nature.

The Christian theological tradition, rooted deeply in the wellsprings of Sacred Scripture, provides just such a language. Today we have come to recognize that "theology is necessarily ecological"[15] – and "ecology is eminently theological by nature."[16] In other words, how we think of God colours our view of the world, and, for the believer, the world cannot be considered apart from the mystery of God.

Responding to the environmental consciousness of our age, we turn now to consider the claim that the Judeo-Christian tradition is to blame for our ecological crisis.[17] Bringing this accusation against our faith communities, critics have focused on biblical texts such as Genesis 1:28, in which humans are reportedly given a mandate to "subdue" the earth and to have "dominion over the fish of the sea and over the birds of the air and over every living thing that moves upon the earth." Suffice it to say that such texts have been grossly misunderstood and have suffered anachronistic interpretations that cite Christianity as the prime ecological culprit.

There is no doubt that strands of the Christian tradition have been ecologically "ambiguous,"[18] but a charge of ecological bankruptcy on the part of Christianity fails to appreciate the diverse creation theologies in Scripture[19] and the rich ecological and cosmic thrust of Christian theology. Sacred Scripture must never be used as a licence for ecological hegemony. However, "the ecologically oriented thesis of Lynn White and others can now be laid to rest," for "rarely, if ever, did pre-modern Jews and Christians construe this verse as a license for the selfish exploitation of the environment."[20] Efforts to blame our present-day environmental crisis on a particular reading of the Bible deflect attention from the widespread human responsibility for our current situation. Worse still, this sort of misnaming of the problem diverts energies from efforts to identify the actual sources of our crisis and to work together to find real solutions.

Our religious traditions, in fact, offer many helpful approaches to the challenge of caring for our planet. Though our faith communities will continue to commit resources to help address the environmental challenges of our age, the religious bodies of the world are unlikely to be the primary authors of the technical solutions to our problems. Our faith traditions serve rather to support a process of conversion directed at an increased sense of *respect, care,* and *love* for our planet. Having learned to love our planet as God's handiwork and the source of life for all creatures, we will feel compelled to seek out the scientific, technical, and social solutions required to save our planet.

An ecological understanding of God

Looking to the Christian theological tradition, I would like to suggest that an ecological reading of the Trinity, that is, an ecological understanding of God, can be used to support the process of conversion required if we are to respond in love to the needs of our wounded planet.

In the Christian tradition, God is revealed as Trinity, as the "central mystery of the Christian faith and life" (*Catechism of the Catholic Church*, no. 234). Through meditations on the Father, Son, and Holy Spirit, and on their relationship to each other, we are drawn into our foundational relationships with God and our neighbour, and with the whole of the created order, which God has declared to be so very good. Following the insights of the German Jesuit theologian Karl Rahner (1904–1984), we are led to recognize the Father, within the Trinity, as the loving and communicating foundation of all that exists. The Father communicates himself ultimately in the history of humanity, and of nature, through the incarnate Son, Jesus Christ. Through the Holy Spirit, God invites and empowers us to live the true meaning of our creation in the image and likeness of God.[21] Our recognition of God as Trinity provides for our meditation an image of perfect unity in relationship. Our experience of God as Trinity invites us to consider all life, and indeed the whole of the natural order, as bound up in relationship with this God who has come to be with us where we live. Becoming aware of these divine relationships and of the generosity of God, respect and care seem an inadequate response. Love, which reaches out continuously to the other, must be our reply to the earth, to our neighbour, and to God, who calls to us in this age of environmental crisis, saying, "What have you done? Your brother's blood cries out to me from the ground!" (Gen. 4:10). The Nicene Creed, a key expression of our faith, also draws out the "ecological" dimensions of the Trinity: God the Father almighty, maker of heaven and earth; Jesus Christ, through whom all things were made; and the Holy Spirit, the Lord, the giver of Life. Let us now consider these different dimensions of our experience of the Triune God.

God the Father, maker of heaven and earth

I believe in one God, the Father almighty,
maker of heaven and earth, of all things visible and
invisible.

According to the American theologian Langdon Gilkey (1919–2004), the idea that God is the creator of all things provides the indispensable foundation upon which the other beliefs of Christianity are based.[22] Creation serves as bookends to the story of salvation. Our biblical salvation narrative is bracketed "in the beginning" by the Genesis stories of creation and at the end time by the Book of Revelation's vision of the new creation. Creation and re-demption become creation and re-creation in and through the love of God.

Used in this context, the term "creation" must be regarded as a theological and not a scientific or philosophical term. This viewpoint cannot be stressed enough. Confusion reigns in contemporary debates on evolution and the Bible, for example, because of the persistent conflation of the term "creation" with "nature." The Christian notion of "creation" does not deal with the scientific questions of origins, per se. The origins of the 4.6-billion-year-old Earth and the 14.7-billon-year-old universe, their evolution, and their future thermodynamic destiny are questions of scientific inquiry. Our theology of creation, however, may be strongly influenced by contemporary scientific accounts or theories about the origin and development of the universe. Acknowledging the gift that science offers our theologies of creation can, in fact, be a liberating experience leading to new and fruitful meditations on God's ways of creation. Nonetheless, our theologies of creation are not intended to speak of God's creation in a scientific way. Theologies of creation speak instead of God's relationship with the natural order; they invite us to grapple with such questions as: Why is there something rather than nothing? Is the world intelligible? Is the world meaningful, now and forever? Classic theological responses to such questions assume God's creative love at the heart of all, God as sustaining ground, and God as ultimate source of eternal meaning. In other words, the world is not simply "out there," devoid of meaning. The theological term "creation" invites us to reflect upon our relationship with the loving and compassionate God who is the foundation of all that is. Scientific considerations of "nature" and "origins" regard the natural world in terms of its own dynamics and not in terms of nature's relationship to God.

Despite the Christian insistence on the relational character of God, the idea of God as Creator sometimes leads to a language that seems to imply that the transcendent God is "out there" over and above creation, with little or nothing to do with creation. This is not what the Christian tradition means by God the Creator. Such false and ultimately sterile notions of God are temptations only when we think of God in categorical terms, as simply one thing or category among the multitude of things we call creation.

God the Creator, however, cannot be viewed as one category or thing among all other things, but rather as the loving ground of all that exists. Creation is revelatory; it is God's gift of "self-bestowal."[23] The God of Abraham is not encountered through philosophical arguments about efficient causality, or as that which causes all else, but rather as the ultimate, constitutive principle of all being, the source and ground of all life, of all that exists.

Other diversions that may arise in our theologies of creation include the claims of pantheism, which regard the world as God, or divine. As well, the world and God are not two separate, irreconcilable realities, as dualism claims; rather, God is present in the world, and the world is present in God.

Jesus Christ – incarnate and cosmic christology

I believe in one Lord Jesus Christ, the Only Begotten Son of God … through him all things were made.

For Christian theology today, the incarnation is a cosmic event, embracing all creation and for all time.[24] The incarnation is the central event of God's self-communication, not only of human history, but of cosmic history. In and through the incarnation, the entire universe is transfigured. It is God who takes on flesh – divine and human natures unite in the Son: the body of Jesus is transfigured to become the fullness of the presence of God in our world and, indeed, in the universe. In turn, the cosmos, by virtue of the incarnation, is made holy. The incarnation appears as "the necessary and permanent beginning of the divinization of the world as a whole."[25]

The New Testament presents a christology – reflections on who and what is Christ – that is cosmic in scope and witnesses to Jesus Christ "in" and "through" whom "all things" were created (1 Cor. 8:6, Col. 1:16, Heb. 1:2, John 1:3) and in whom "all things" will be transformed (Col. 1:20, Eph.

1:10, Heb. 1:3). This witness places Christ at the very heart of the evolving universe.[26] Jesus Christ is indeed the alpha and the omega, the beginning and the end – through him, with him, and in him, all things are created. No wonder that Pope John Paul II, in his final encyclical, *Ecclesia de Eucharistia*, on the Eucharist, could boldly claim that the Eucharist is a cosmic event, celebrated on the altar of the world, uniting heaven and earth and permeating all creation (EE, no. 9).

In this vision, Jesus Christ is indeed the Lord and Saviour of all creation, and worthy of our worship. In fact, we can boldly proclaim that all creation is inherently Christic. Creation is never simply the stage upon which our salvation is enacted, but rather the very heart of Christ's creative and redemptive act. Furthermore, the resurrection of Christ fulfills the promise that all things would be gathered up in Christ (Eph. 1:8-10). In the resurrection of Christ, the destiny of the world is already in principle decided and has already begun.[27] From the perspective of God, Jesus Christ is God's self-communication to the world. This is the most significant event in history. From the perspective of creation, Jesus Christ is the self-transcendence of the universe into God.

God the Holy Spirit – the indwelling of Creation

I believe in the Holy Spirit, the Lord, the giver of life ...

God is "at home" in his creation, in and through the life-giving, animating, sustaining action of the Spirit. In this fashion, creation is regarded as being imbued with a hidden dimension of God. Creation is never static, never devoid of God's animating grace. God is always present to the world, prompting it to transcend itself, to go beyond itself. Creation is *creatio continua*, that is, it is moving forward, emerging, and evolving in the grace of God. The universe, all creation, is moving towards God. This is the goal of history.

The Spirit calls the cosmos into continuous being, empowering the universe from within, inviting the universe into the future. The emergence of novelty, the dynamic of evolutionary chance and necessity may be viewed as "driven" or "invited" by the Spirit. In this light, the evolution-creation conflict is a false dichotomy for a Christian. Only one world exists, the created world of God.

In our present age, however, we have come to use different languages to speak of this one created world. Considering the diversity and connectedness of life in our world, science speaks rightly of evolutionary processes. Theology speaks rather of the immanent, vivifying Spirit at the heart of creation and of the cosmos as the temple of the Holy Spirit. As believers we have come to understand the cosmos, and indeed all life, as expressions of the immanent Spirit at work, labouring, nurturing, inviting, and loving into existence. The Spirit is thus rightly described as the giver of life.

God as dynamic, Trinitarian communion

We have examined each "person" of the Trinity from an ecological perspective. We know that God is fully expressed in each of the Father, the Son, and the Holy Spirit. At the same time, God has been revealed to us as Trinitarian. As we are beginning to see, this doctrine of the Trinity has important ecological implications. We also recognize that theologies of the Trinity can contribute significantly to a religiously inspired awareness of our connectedness through God to the whole of creation.

God may be described as a God of communion, as a Trinity of persons in communion. Various theologians have characterized the Trinity by suggesting that each divine person relates to the other as mutual love (lover, beloved, love), communion, or unity in love. In other words, God's "to-be" is "to-be-in-relationship."

The relational, loving mutuality inherent in God has significant implications for how we view the rest of the created order. According to the Australian Catholic theologian Denis Edwards, "if the Creator's being is radically relational, then this suggests [that] the very being of things in our universe is relational being."[28] God the Father acts as the source of both intra-trinitarian and extra-trinitarian communications. Internally, the fertile, self-expressive love of the Father leads, via the generation of the Son and the Spirit, to the plurality we call the Trinity, where three are indeed one. Externally, the triune God's life-giving and life-sustaining love overflows and explodes into the diversity of creation, into the world of biodiversity and the many and varied expressions of the earth's ecosystems and processes.[29]

Sacramentality of creation

Today we recognize that our Catholic theology is fundamentally sacramental. In other words, we tend to discover and experience something of the divine both in and through our experience of creation. Our grasp of the Trinity as an expression of God's mutual, indwelling love, and of creation as a manifestation of that love, leads to an understanding of creation as revelatory. Nature, under-stood in its religious sense as the created order, is regarded as God's handiwork, the Book of Life.

St. Bonaventure reads creation as a book of revelation, as a reflection of the Trinitarian life, as a manifestation of God. For Bonaventure, "the universe is like a book reflecting, representing, and describing its Maker, the Trinity, at three different levels of expression: as a trace, an image and a likeness."[30] Every creature acts as a trace of God. Intellectual creatures act as image of God, and God-conformed creatures act as likeness of God. Nature is not simply a collection of things "out there," devoid of any meaning, but rather a pregnant manifestation of the dynamic, interior life of the Trinity. Nature is, therefore, an expression of the Trinity possessing an intrinsic capacity to draw us back to God.

Redemption of Creation – An Eschatology

Our traditional notions of the so-called end times have, for the most part, considered only the destiny of the human person. Christianity has tended to be concerned with an "individual eschatology" focusing on questions relating to human death, salvation, damnation, resurrection, and the beatific vision. We now recognize that this individual, anthropocentric focus is only part of the picture. Karl Rahner directs us to consider the terms traditionally used to describe humankind's final and definitive state, including those relating to our personal salvation, the immortality of the soul, and the resurrection of the flesh, as terms "de-scribing a final and definitive state of fulfillment for the cosmos."[31] In this reflection we remember that St. Paul has declared that "when everything has been subjected to him, then the Son himself will be subjected to the One who has subjected everything to him, so that God may be all in all" (1 Cor. 15:28).

Christian reflection on the destiny of humankind, or eschatology, that is true to its name includes all creation in its understanding of final salvation and meaning in God.[32] All things are created in God, sustained by God, and brought to final redemption in God. Nothing is left out in God's infinite mercy and love.

As human beings, we are embodied spirits, an intimate unity of body and soul. As individuals and as a species, we may be regarded as icons of the general spirit-matter unity of all creation. Aware of the experience of death that connects us to all other living creatures, we affirm the resurrection of Jesus Christ to be the beginning sign of the eschatological hope of the entire creation. Such is the hope that grounds the future promise of all in Christ and his resurrection.

Catholic social teaching and the environment

Concern for the poor and concern for nature are integral features of modern Catholic thought. As a result of certain historic tensions between social activists and environmentalists, the truth of this assertion has not always been obvious. Care for the earth may have, in the past, been regarded by some social activists as a distraction in the face of seemingly insurmountable issues of human rights, migration and refugees, poverty and hunger. Today, the vision of Catholic social activists and environmentalists has come together with that of other people of goodwill who recognize that the poor are "unequally burdened" by the impoverishment of the earth's ecological services, such as clean water and productive soils. The consequences of this vision may be seen in the 2011–2016 education program for the Canadian Catholic Organization for Development and Peace that focuses on ecological justice.[33]

A Christian vision of ecology must, therefore, include both concern for the poor and the marginalized and concern for nature and biodiversity. Pope John Paul II has stated that "the proper ecological balance will not be found without *directly addressing the structural forms of poverty that exist throughout the world.*"[34] The Canadian Conference of Catholic Bishops amplifies this papal concern by stating that "the cry of the earth and the cry of the poor are one" and that "ecological harmony cannot exist in a world of unjust social structures; nor can the extreme social inequalities ... result in ecological sustainability."[35]

Pope John Paul II's 1990 World Day of Peace Message was the first comprehensive papal document dedicated solely to ecology and has proved to be widely influential. Papal concern for the environment began in the early years after the Second Vatican Council[36] and continued in the writings and allocutions of Pope Benedict XVI.[37]

A rich tradition of church teaching on ecology and human development has grown over the past three decades. In response to pressing socio-ecological issues, individual bishops and episcopal conferences have issued pastoral letters on ecology. One of the earliest pastoral letters on ecology was written by the Philippine Bishops (*What is Happening to Our Beautiful Land: A Pastoral Letter on Ecology, 1988*).[38] Recent letters include those written on the

Great Barrier Reef (2004) by the Bishops of Queensland[39] and on the Athabasca Oil Sands (2009) by the Bishop of St. Paul, Alberta.[40] Many of these documents have not been given the attention they deserve.

The Anthropocene: Science and faith in partnership

There exists only one world, one planet Earth. The photograph known as "Earthrise," taken by the astronauts of the Apollo 8 mission in 1968, has helped to illustrate for us the real limits of our planet. The traditions of science and religion can, together, lead us to a new understanding of how we must respond to the dire state of Earth with all its beauty, richness, and limits. Scientists need to hear from theologians, and theologians need to hear from scientists. As Pope John Paul II expressed in his letter to the Director of the Vatican Observatory, "Science can purify religion from error and superstition; religion can purify science from idolatry and false absolutes. Each can draw the other into a wider world, a world in which both can flourish."[41]

Given the current state of the global ecological crisis, we are all aware of the need for collaborative efforts between the forces of science and religion. Where once religious language and traditions were cited by some as the problem, or even the "cause" of the environmental crisis, we now recognize that "there are no solutions to the systemic causes of ecocrisis ... apart from religious narrative."[42] Science, as well as technology, economics, and politics, are absolutely necessary, though they will never be sufficient to inspire and animate our response to the cry of the earth and the cry of the poor. Our response must, instead, be grounded upon an understanding that succeeds in convincing our minds and moving our hearts. Scientifically based appraisals of the state of our planetary ecosystems will necessarily inform our decision making, but they cannot alone decide for us what constitutes the good. Nor is science likely to produce the level of empathy, conversion, and action that the current environmental crisis should elicit from us.

The ecological crisis is not, therefore, primarily a scientific, economic, or technological crisis. It is, rather, a moral crisis, a cultural crisis, a spiritual crisis. It speaks to our most deeply held values regarding the created world and our sense of our place in that world. What we need is not an ethic per se, but rather an ethos; not a program, but a change of heart. We need a religious language that speaks to that conversion or metanoia.

Only a discourse that includes the voices of religion can offer what is really needed to meet the ecological challenge. Whether we seek a new morality, a new culture, or a sense of the deeply personal and sacred character of creation, we are longing for what only religion can provide. Authentic religion invites us to a holy vision that embraces the fullness of God's creation, to a personal and social conversion, a dying to ourselves so that all creation may live and flourish. We seek a re-enchantment of nature as the word and beauty of God.

It may be that only by becoming contemplatives, that is, by living as mystics conformed by grace to Christ, will we have the eyes to see and the ears to hear the call of God to fullness of life. But this has been the invitation held out to us throughout our journey with God. "I have set before you life and death ... Choose life so that you and your descendants may live" (Deut. 30:19). "I have come that you may have life and life to the full (John 10:10). Yes, life to the full, which God, in Jesus Christ and the Spirit, bestows on us with unbounded generosity and unfailing love.

Chapter 5

FAITH AND THE EARTH: PART II

Les Miller

Les Miller is an instructor of Religious Education at OISE, University of Toronto. He was a teacher, Chaplaincy Team Leader, and Department Head in both Dufferin-Peel and York Catholic District School Boards. From 1999 until 2010, he served as Consultant and then Coordinator of Religious Education with York Catholic District School Board. He has been involved in curriculum development for schools (Elementary and Secondary Curriculum Religious Education Guidelines), AQ and pre-service courses with the Institute for Catholic Education. He contributed to the Canadian Bishops Grade 12 *In Search of the Good* program. More recently, as part of the Nelson/Novalis team, he helped to create *World Religions: A Canadian Catholic Perspective*. Les is author or co-author of seventeen published books in the area of Religious Education including the *25 Questions* series and the *Words for the Journey* prayer books.

I n preparing teachers for the classroom, I am frequently challenged to resolve the apparent controversies surrounding Catholic teaching and science. Frequently, these future high school science teachers wonder if one can be a good scientist and a good Catholic. I respond in the affirmative, citing examples of Catholic scientists and pointing to ways of approaching the difficult issues that threaten the survival of life on this planet. To begin, however, we need to consider some of the ways that faith and science relate.

The relationship between science and religion

Ian Barbour taught for many years at Carleton University in the departments of physics and religion. In one of his most famous books, *When Science Meets Religion*, he speaks of four models for the interaction between science and religion: conflict, independence, dialogue, and integration.

The first model, *conflict*, is where science and religion battle against each other in creating meaning systems. In this model, there is no grey area: if one is true, then the other is necessarily false. The Galileo affair is an example of this way of interacting. So, too, is the current debate between evolutionists and creationists. Evolutionists of an atheistic persuasion, such as Richard Dawkins, argue that the fact of evolution is indisputable and that the biblical story of how things came to be is utter nonsense.

Creationists, who tend to read the Bible literally, consider that evolutionary science is simply untrue because it does not agree with the creation accounts in the Book of Genesis. The starting points of the two sides are so diametrically opposed that any meaningful conversation is impossible.

A second model, *independence*, describes religion and science as having separate ways of knowing, with different questions, methods, and concerns. Perhaps the best-known exponent of this model is Stephen Jay Gould, the late Harvard scientist and evolutionary theorist. Essentially, Gould argues that both science and faith possess "non-overlapping magisteria" that speak with authority in their own specific areas of expertise and knowledge, and these areas are distinct: boundaries between the two are not to be blurred. Science asks the "how" questions, while religion deals with the "why" of it all. This model seems to present a pair of intellectual silos that seldom, if ever, interact. In everyday life, adherence to this model can be a challenge for Catholic scientists who see creation, with its complexity and beauty, as a revelation of God and a source of spiritual strength. Nonetheless, this is likely a very popular model, since it avoids the negativity associated with the conflict model.

The third model proposed by Barbour is a *dialogue* approach. The key idea here is one of respectful conversation between two parties, each having expertise and authority in its own field, but wanting to understand better the point of view of the other. Science can pose questions that it does not have the tools to answer on its own. These questions may be metaphysical or moral. Similarly, religion can pose questions about factual data that it is not equipped to deal with. When it comes to the earth's survival, for example, religion cannot answer questions about the extent of climate change, carbon sinks, and the impact of strip mining on an ecosystem. But it can address the ethical and moral dimensions of these issues. To further understanding, science and religion work together, with science addressing the "is" and religion the "ought."

The fourth approach is the *integration* or *reconciliation* model. Science and religion can coexist in harmony, says Barbour, because both are on a quest to discover truth. There is indeed sufficient overlap that each perspective can shed light on certain aspects of the other. Pope John Paul II, in a letter to Fr. George Coyne of the Vatican Observatory, underscores this fourth model by noting that "science can purify religion from error and superstition; religion can purify science from idolatry and false absolutes. Each can draw the other into a wider world, a world in which both can flourish."[1]

In an interview on the PBS television program *Nova*, biologist Ken Miller, a Brown University professor well known for his opposition to creationism, reflected on his Catholic faith and his vocation as a scientist. He sees faith and reason as gifts from God – gifts that do not contradict one another. Scientific reason, he says, has allowed us to explore the world around us and to come to an appreciation that it is far older and more complex than anyone could have imagined. But this ability to analyze nature doesn't make it any less of a mystery. As he puts it, "In a way it deepens our faith and our appreciation for the author of that nature, the author of that physical universe. And to people of faith, that author is God." For the religious person to truly understand the world in which we live, argues Miller, both faith and scientific reason are necessary.[2]

The Catholic Church clearly respects the role of science and technology in finding solutions to the many problems, including ecological problems, that beset the earth and all its inhabitants. Although the relationship between science and faith may be challenging, Pope John Paul II stressed the privileged position of scientists in their explorations. Scientists search for the truth, and God is the ultimate truth. "Seen from this point of view, science shines forth in all its value as a good capable of motivating an existence, as a great experience of freedom for truth, as a fundamental work of service. Through it, each researcher feels that he is able himself to grow, and to help others to grow, in humanity."[3] Scientific inquiry is thus a way of entering into the mystery that is God, and also a path of moral service to others and to the planet. Science, therefore, can make an enormous contribution to the healing of a wounded world.

This belief was highlighted once again in 2002, when Pope John Paul II and Patriarch Bartholomew of Constantinople signed a joint Declaration on the Environment. They agreed on several goals, including one that points to the constructive harmony of science and faith: "Science may help us to correct the mistakes of the past, in order to enhance the spiritual and material well-being of the present and future generations."[4]

At the same time, however, the Catholic Church does not embrace technology – the practical application of science – uncritically. Nor does it embrace the Luddite mentality of resisting technological innovation out of fear of change. But the Church does ask that people temper scientific applications with wisdom and morality.

The Second Vatican Council (1962–1965) emphasized the complementarity of science and religion – both seek the truth. One of the Council documents, *Gaudium et Spes*, is a hope-filled description of how the Church can interact with modern culture, of which scientific activity is an integral part. Section 36 is particularly relevant. It stresses that scientific research that is respectful of and guided by moral norms "never truly conflicts with faith, for earthly matters and the concerns of faith derive from the same God." Indeed, the document deplores the closed-mindedness of those who insist that science and religion can only relate in a conflictual way: "We cannot but deplore certain habits of mind, which are sometimes found too among Christians, which do not sufficiently attend to the rightful independence of science and which, from the arguments and controversies they spark, lead many minds to conclude that faith and science are mutually opposed" (GS, no. 36).

The contemporary mindset

Many of us are immersed in a wired world replete with gadgets and thinking patterns that reveal our dependence on technology. The digital age changes our human nature. We communicate, work, and play much differently than our grandparents did. Nuclear physicist Ursula Franklin warns that we need to be aware of the ways technology can shape our moral values and patterns of thinking. This technology pervades our lives both materially and culturally. As she so aptly puts it, "Technology has built the house in which we all live … Today there is hardly any human activity that does not occur within this house." For better or for worse, we are a changed species.

Charles Taylor, the Canadian philosopher, would concur. He has written persuasively about a contemporary mindset that has developed over the past two centuries. He calls it instrumental reason. "By 'instrumental reason' I mean the kind of rationality we draw on when we calculate the most economical application of means to a given end. Maximum efficiency, the best cost-output ratio, is its measure of success."[5] This observation resonates with French Catholic philosopher Gabriel Marcel's contention that our life threatens to become a series of problems to be solved rather than mysteries to be embraced. Taylor specifically critiques excessive dependence on technology because it may divert our attention from the fact that another type of solution may be more appropriate. He argues that we can become so enamoured of the technological approach in medicine, for instance, that the patient simply becomes an object requiring a technical solution rather than a "whole person with a life story." This focus can also blind us to other resources at our disposal, specifically nurses "who more often than not provide this humanly sensitive caring, as against that of specialists with high-tech knowledge."[6]

Taylor is not speaking as a Luddite; rather, he is warning about an excessive dependence on technology in tackling human problems. Similarly, in his 2009 encyclical *Caritas et Veritate*, Pope Benedict XVI drew our attention to the current overemphasis on technique at the expense of questions of morality and faith. This is not a good thing. "Technological development can give rise to the idea that technology is self-sufficient when too much attention is given to the 'how' questions, and not enough to the many 'why' questions underlying human activity" (CV, no. 70).

Martin Luther King, Jr., on the occasion of his acceptance of the Nobel Peace Prize, articulated the call for science to work with morality and spirituality. The world has seen spectacular achievements in science and technology, but in some ways the resulting material benefits have not made us better people. In his view, "We have learned to fly the air like birds and swim the sea like fish, but we have not learned the simple art of living together as brothers [and sisters]."[7] For King, the issue was the lack of balance.

Clearly, there is an important role for science and technology today, but there is also need to discern the balance between modes of addressing problems. Yes, we need science, but we also need compassion and justice. With regard to ecological issues, we clearly need to find technical solutions, but we also need to stand in awe and wonder at the intricacy, harmony, and beauty of creation.

Ecological conversion

Human attitudes and habits have had a harmful impact on nature. Indeed, we have wounded our planet as our scientific knowledge has outstripped the understanding and wisdom needed to make technological applications appropriately serve the greater good. Pope John Paul II addressed this issue with his call for an "ecological conversion" in a general audience on January 17, 2001. He pointed to a heritage where two contrasting governance roles have affected the human relationship with creation. The first has been that of the autonomous despot who exploits creation for selfish, short-sighted ends. Nature is seen exclusively as a resource to be exploited as efficiently as possible. This leads to scarring of the landscape, reduced biodiversity, and contaminated waters and skies. The second stance is that of ministry. A minister is one who serves. Humanity is called to serve creation: "It is not the mission of an absolute and uncensurable master, but of a minister of the Kingdom of God, called to continue the work of the Creator, a work of life and peace. His responsibility, defined in the Book of Wisdom, is to govern the world 'in holiness and justice.'"[8] In this context, the Pope called for an ecological conversion – a fundamental shift in attitude about creation and the consequent behaviours that reduce the harmful human impacts on it.

This is a conversion of perception towards the place of humanity within nature. We are called to reclaim a heritage of stewardship of creation that can be traced from Genesis, in which God commissioned Adam to care for the Garden of Eden: "The Lord God took the man and put him in the garden of Eden to till it and keep it" (Gen. 2:15). St. Francis of Assisi famously called elements of nature his brothers and sisters in the *Canticle of the Sun*. Stewardship of creation is named as a core Catholic social teaching in many compendia in recent years. Recently, the Canadian Conference of Catholic Bishops published two pastoral letters that draw out the implications of ecological conversion for Canadians: *The Christian Ecological Imperative* (2003)[9] and *Our Relationship with the Environment: The Need for Conversion* (2008).[10] In Scripture (Gen. 1:28), God tells humankind to subdue the earth. Catholic teaching is clear about what "subdue" means, and it has nothing to do with arbitrary and destructive behaviour. To the contrary, the *Catechism of the Catholic Church* says, "God calls man and woman, made in the image of the Creator 'who loves everything that exists,' to share in his providence toward other creatures; hence their responsibility for the world God has been entrusted to them" (CCC, no. 373).

Ecological issues as spiritual issues

Ecology has to do with the relations of organisms to one another and to their physical surroundings. Human ecology refers more directly to the interaction of people with their environment. So what is the relationship between ecology and spirituality?

Spirituality has to do with our relationship to God, with our personal experience of God's presence in our life, and our resulting way of living and relationship to other people. A specifically Christian spirituality has to do with living life "according to the spirit" of the risen Jesus, as St. Paul would say (Rom. 8:5), and with the knowledge that we can communicate intimately with the God whom Jesus addressed as Abba. As one writer puts it, "Spirituality is concerned with the lifestyle that is opened up as a result of the interaction between God and human beings."[11] Or, to put it another way, a Christian's experience of a personal relationship with God should have consequences for how we relate to others – and to the entire created order, which is imbued with the hidden presence of God in some mysterious way; hence the expression "the integrity of creation" and the expectation that we treat all created reality with the respect that is its due. To relate disrespectfully to our environment and all it contains is hardly consistent with Christian spirituality's relational, healing, and reconciling focus.

Pope John Paul II uses the language of conversion to approach ecological issues. Science and technology have given us alternatives to carbon and nuclear energy in the form of renewable energy sources. It is not enough to know technological solutions to ecological difficulties; the desire to make these changes is also needed. As the British scientist John Houghton says, "Not having the will is a spiritual problem, not a scientific problem."[12]

Sacred Scripture, especially the psalms and the gospels, repeatedly calls us to look at nature to draw closer to God. For Christians, creation is a revelation of the sacred. Desecrating the earth through ecological contamination conceals God. "God's glory is revealed in the natural world, yet we humans are presently destroying creation. In this light, the ecological crisis is also a profoundly religious crisis. In destroying creation we are limiting our ability to know and love God."[13] Hence, ecological issues are also spiritual issues.

The ethical dimension of ecological issues

Advances in technologies can be ethically problematic: the development of genetically modified crops or the use of growth hormones in meat may have negative consequences for both the environment and human health. On the other hand, "benevolent innovation," such as clean energy production or the microbial degradation of pollutants, can mitigate climate change.[14]

Christian ethics asks how ought we to respond, what ought we to do, in light of the gospel of Jesus Christ and the Church's reflection on that gospel, when we are confronted with the mistreatment of nature, the consequences of which are manifesting themselves most particularly in the negative and often devastating effects of climate change.

The Church has been explicit in its call for justice for the earth. In fact, over twenty years ago, Pope John Paul II called for direct action to reduce the effects of atmospheric deterioration and the depletion of the ozone layer due to growing industrialization, urbanization, and energy consumption: "Industrial waste, the burning of fossil fuels, unrestricted deforestation, the use of certain types of herbicides, coolants and propellants: all of these are known to harm the atmosphere and environment. The resulting meteorological and atmospheric changes range from damage to health to the possible future submersion of low-lying lands."[15]

A technological fix solves problems by applying the best scientific thinking to human issues. And this can be effective. When the Deepwater Horizon oil platform exploded in 2010 in the Gulf of Mexico, scientists and engineers eventually found technical solutions to stop oil, which had been contaminating the ecosystems over thousands of square kilometres, from leaking into the Gulf. They responded to this problem by finding innovative ways of stemming the flow of the oil some 1500 metres below sea level. They also sought ways of cleaning beaches and wildlife caught in the escaped oil.

The alarm bells were sounding, however, and many voices were raised to question what was actually happening. They stressed other solutions that called for different ways of behaving so that we no longer feel compelled to drill for oil in precarious situations. They argued for an attitudinal fix that changes perceptions and behaviours to prevent such catastrophes. Harking back to the days of the Exxon Valdez oil spill in 1989, Greenpeace published in newspapers around the world an advertisement with a picture of the oil tanker's captain and the following message: "It wasn't his driving that caused the Alaskan oil spill. It was yours."

Integrating technological and attitudinal fixes is clearly required to meet enormous challenges such as climate change. Technological fixes can reduce greenhouse gases being emitted from cars and factories, while attitudinal fixes can lead to many conservation strategies that help us reduce our consumption of products that contribute to global warming. But the attitudinal fix, while necessary, is still insufficient. Ecological issues are moral issues calling for sustained ethical reflection, in the light of faith, that help us – the Christian community – to discern what God is inspiring and requiring that we be and do, now and in the future.

This process of reflection, however, does not always lead to black-and-white answers. Despite the grave concerns over climate change and other ecological issues, for example, the Vatican has not made definitive statements about the use of different forms of energy. It has called for prudence, wisdom, and consideration for future generations in making energy choices. The seventh commandment tells people that theft is sinful. In that context, the *Catechism of the Catholic Church* argues that we should not steal from our descendants. Our use of the world's resources "cannot be divorced from respect for moral imperatives ... It requires a religious respect for the integrity of creation" (CCC, no. 2415).

This kind of respect has led bishops in different dioceses, assemblies, and conferences around the world to bring different energy projects under scrutiny. The Auxiliary Bishop of Osaka, Bishop Michael Goro Matsuura, for example, has spoken out against Japan's nuclear program in the wake of the serious accident at Fukushima plant in March 2011. Similarly, Alberta's bishops have called for prudence in building nuclear plants in their province. Serious ethical questions need addressing before approving such options.

The Alberta oil sands and the Catholic Church

A closer examination of the Catholic approach to challenges posed by extracting oil exemplifies much of what has been written in this chapter. In 2009, Bishop Luc Bouchard of the Diocese of St. Paul, Alberta, wrote a pastoral letter questioning the wisdom of the rapid development of Alberta's oil sands. For decades, the potential of extracting oil from its sandy matrix has been explored by scientists and engineers. Ways of separating oil from the sand particles were found by exploiting an intermediate film of water that surrounded the sand underneath the oil layer. The difficulty lay in the heating of the water. This required other energy. Natural gas has proved to be the most effective. Processing of this oil adds to greenhouse gases in two ways: in the actual processing operation and in the burning of the oil products at their destinations.

Climate scientists have warned about the catastrophic potential of rising global temperatures. There are other questions about suitable treatment of the extensive waste products and the amount of water needed to make extraction feasible and the consequent effects on communities downstream. The reserves in the Alberta oil sands are the second largest in the world. This has enormous economic and political significance for Canada and the United States. Development of these resources will add to Canadian economic prosperity and make North America less dependent on oil coming from around the world. Oil produced in the Middle East, Nigeria, Russia, and Venezuela involves trading with countries beset by uncertain and sometimes antagonistic politics. Hence, oil companies, along with the Alberta and Canadian governments, have all advocated quick development of these resources based on technological, economic, and political considerations.

Bishop Bouchard nonetheless calls for a slower and more prudent approach to the development of these resources. He largely builds his argument on Chapter 10 of the *Compendium of the Social Doctrine of the Church*, entitled "Safeguarding the Environment."[16] He traces a line of ecological stewardship already mentioned in this chapter. He also quoted Pope Benedict XVI on the interdependence of human, social, and natural ecology:

"Alongside the ecology of nature there exists what can be called a 'human' ecology, which in turn demands a 'social' ecology. All this means that humanity, if it truly desires peace, must be increasingly conscious of the links between natural ecology, or respect for nature, and human ecology. Experience shows that *disregard for the environment always harms human coexistence* and vice versa."[17]

In other words, ecology from a scientific perspective has been applied to cultural and spiritual dimensions of life. Everything is connected and everything is interdependent. From a Catholic perspective, science takes place in a social, moral, and spiritual context. Scientific and technological work on the oil sands has vast implications. The issues are not just scientific, economic, and political; they are also religious. The development of the oil sands is having a profound cultural impact. Fort McMurray has become a boom town with attendant social problems. Activity in the oil sands is also disruptive to First Nations communities in northern Alberta. While some embrace the possibility of prosperity, others fear health impacts as well as environmental disruptions.

Bishop Bouchard argues that the integrity of creation has been a secondary consideration to economic gain and that further oil sands development constitutes "a serious moral problem." The air, water, and forests of the Athabasca oil sands region must be protected by government and industry, says the bishop. Siding with environmentalists and the First Nations and Métis people, he bluntly concludes that "the present pace and scale of development in the Athabasca oil sands cannot be morally justified. Active steps to alleviate this environmental damage must be undertaken."[18]

Bishop Bouchard's call for answers to serious environmental and social questions shows the interconnectedness of scientific and technological enterprises with morality, spirituality, and culture. This model calls on scientists to transcend the narrow parameters of their work in solving particular problems and ask deep questions about the impact of their work on the earth and on the social and spiritual landscape.

Science and faith as partners

Although science and religion have different questions and approaches, they share a common concern for the survival and thriving of a healthy planet. From a Catholic perspective, knowledge entails responsibility. An excellent summary of the Catholic approach to teaching science is found in the Course Profile produced for the Grade 9 Applied Science Course in Ontario:

> Science and technology are fruits of the human intellect. Advances in both science and technology have done much to further our understanding of the world in which we live. As students of science, we cannot help but marvel with wonder and awe (gifts of the Holy Spirit) at the miraculous nature of the universe. As stewards of the earth, we must make sure that both science and technology work to enhance life on the planet. We now know how interdependent the inanimate (non-living) and animate (living) parts of the biosphere are. As caretakers, we must recognize that the exploitation of resources endangers the delicate balance of life. It is our responsibility to make sure that when we extract minerals and metals from the earth that we do not destroy the local ecosystem. We must also be aware that the by-products (pollutants) of our industrial processes pose a significant threat to life. We must safeguard the local and global environments from the toxic effects of pollutants.
>
> As human persons, we have a special obligation to other people in the world (solidarity). In the story of Cain and Abel (Genesis 4:9) we hear the ques-

tion: Am I my brother's/sister's keeper? The answer is a resounding yes. We must make sure that we ask certain questions each time we are deciding on the value of an application of science. How will this contribute to the greater good of humanity? How will this benefit the poor? Does this threaten the life-sustaining capacity of the earth?[19]

Endnotes

Chapter 1

1   C. S. Lewis, *The Discarded Image (1964; Cambridge: Cambridge University Press, 1994)*, 116.

2   Ibid., 216.

3   Brian Purfield, "The Letter to the Colossans: Jesus and the Universe," http://www.thinkingfaith.org/articles/20090623_1.htm.

4   G. K. Chesterton, *Orthodoxy* (1908; San Francisco: Ignatius Press, 1995), 158.

5   Letter from Jefferson to Andrew Ellicott, quoted in John G. Burke, *Cosmic Debris: Meteorites in History* (Berkeley: University of California Press, 1986), 56.

Chapter 2

1   This creation account, the so-called Priestly account, will be referred to as the "first" creation story of the Book of Genesis (Gen. 1:1–2:4a). Here, the reference to "first" is used in relation to its appearance in the book of Genesis. The Yahwist account of creation that comes second (Gen. 2:4b-25) actually predates the Priestly account.

2   For an excellent overview and analysis of the biblical stories of creation, see Raymond E. Brown, Joseph A. Fitzmyer, and Roland E. Murphy, eds., *The New Jerome Biblical Commentary* (1968; Toronto: Novalis, 2011).

3   Meeting of the Holy Father Benedict XVI with the Clergy of the Dioceses of Belluno-Feltre and Treviso, 24 July 2007. http://www.vatican.va/holy_father/benedict_xvi/speeches/2007/july/documents/hf_ben-xvi_spe_20070724_clero-cadore_en.html

4   Pope John Paul II, "Truth Cannot Contradict Truth," Address to the Pontifical Academy of Sciences, 22 October 1996. http://www.newadvent.org/library/docs_jp02tc.htm, a. 4.

5   For the complete proceedings of the Plenary Session, see http://www.casinapioiv.va/content/accademia/en/publications/acta/evolution.html

6   Pope Benedict XVI, Address of His Holiness Benedict XVI to Members of the Pontifical Academy of Sciences on the Occasion of their Plenary Assembly, 31 October 2008. http://www.vatican.va/holy_fathcr/beuedict_xvi/speeches/2008/october/documents/hf_ben-xvi_spe_20081031_academy-sciences_en.html

7   Ibid.

8   Ibid.

9   International Theological Commission (ITC), "Communion and Stewardship: Human Persons Created in the Image of God," *Origins* 34, no. 15 (2004): a. 66.

10 Pope John Paul II, "Truth Cannot Contradict Truth," a. 5.

11 Cornelia Dean, "Science of the Soul? 'I Think, Therefore I Am' Is Losing Force," *The New York Times*, 26 June 2007. http://www.nytimes.com/2007/06/26/science/26soul.html?pagewanted=1

12 Ibid.

13 Pope John Paul II, Address to the Pontifical Academy of Sciences, 10 November 2003. http://www.vatican.va/holy_father/john_paul_ii/speeches/2003/november/documents/hf_jp-ii_spe_20031110_academy-sciences_en.html

Chapter 3

1   Francis S. Collins. *The Language of God* (New York: Free Press, 2006), 228.

2   World Council of Churches, Faith and Order Commission, "Christian Perspectives on Theological Anthropology" Faith and Order Paper 199, 2004.

3   Charles Cameron. "An Introduction to 'Theological Anthropology,'" *Evangel* 23.2 (Summer 2005): 54.

4   Ibid., 59.

Chapter 4

1   Paul J. Crutzen, "Geology of Mankind," *Nature* 415, no. 6867 (2002): 23.

2   Will Steffen et al., "The Anthropocene: Conceptual and Historical Perspectives," *Philosophical Transactions of the Royal Society A* 369(2011): 842–67.

3   Erle C. Ellis, "Anthropocentric Transformation of the Terrestrial Biosphere," *Philosophical Transactions of the Royal Society A* 369(2011): 1010–35.

4   Paul L. Koch and Anthony D. Barnosky, "Late Quarternary Extinctions: State of the Debate," *Annual Review of Ecology, Evolution and Systematics* 37(2006): 215–50.

5   Erle C. Ellis et al., "Anthropogenic Transformation of the Biomes, 1700 to 2000," *Global Ecology and Biogeography* 19(2010).

6   Erle C. Ellis and Navin Ramankutty, "Putting People in the Map: Anthropogenic Biomes of the World," *Frontiers in Ecology and the Environment* 6, no. 8 (2008): 439–47.

7   Millennium Ecosystem Assessment, "Living Beyond Our Means: Natural Assets and Human Well-Being, Statement from the Board," (2005), 5. Report available at http://www.maweb.org/documents/document.429. aspx.pdf.

8   Ibid.

9   Joel E. Cohen, "Human Population: The Next Half Century," *Science* 302, no. 5648 (2003): 1172–75.

10 David E. Bloom, "7 Billion and Counting," *Science* 333, no. 6042 (2011): 562–69.

11 United Nations Environment Programme, *Global Environment Outlook (Geo 4): Summary for Decision Makers* (2007), 6. Report available at http://www.unep.org/geo/geo4/media/GEO4%20SDM_launch.pdf.

12 Mathis Wackernagel and William Rees, *Our Ecological Footprint: Reducing Human Impact on the Earth* (Gabriola Island, BC: New Society Press, 1996).

13 Millennium Ecosystem Assessment, 2005.

14 World Wildlife Fund Report produced in collaboration with Global Footprint Network and Zoological Society of London, "Living Planet Report 2012: Biodiversity, Biocapacity and Better Choices," (2012), 40. Report available at http://awsassets.panda.org/downloads/1_lpr_2012_ online_full_size_single_pages_final_120516.pdf.

15 Denis Edwards, *Jesus the Wisdom of God: An Ecological Theology* (Eugene, OR: Wipf & Stock, 2005), 2.

16 Leonardo Boff, *Ecology and Liberation: A New Paradigm* (Maryknoll, NY: Orbis Books, 1995), 11.

17 Lynn White, Jr., "The Historical Roots of Our Ecologic Crisis," *Science* 155, no. 3767 (1967).

18 H. Paul Santmire, *The Travail of Nature: The Ambiguous Ecological Promise of Christian Theology* (Philadelphia: Fortress Press, 1985).

19 William P. Brown, *The Seven Pillars of Creation: The Bible, Science, and the Ecology of Wonder* (New York: Oxford University Press, 2010).

20 Jeremy Cohen, *"Be Fertile and Increase, Fill the Earth and Master It": The Ancient and Medieval Career of a Biblical Text* (Ithaca: Cornell University Press, 1989), 5.

21 Karl Rahner, *Foundations of Christian Faith: An Introduction to the Idea of Christianity,* trans. William V. Dych (New York: Seabury Press, 1978), 136.

22 Langdon Gilkey, *Maker of Heaven and Earth: The Christian Doctrine of Creation in the Light of Modern Knowledge* (Lanham: University Press of America, 1985), 4.

23 Michael W. Petty, *A Faith that Loves the Earth: The Ecological Theology of Karl Rahner* (Lanham, MD: University Press of America, 1996), 102.

24 Ibid., 132–36.

25 Rahner, *Foundations of Christian Faith,* 181.

26 Ilia Delio, *Christ in Evolution* (Maryknoll, NY: Orbis Books, 2008).

27 Karl Rahner, "Resurrection," in *Encyclopedia of Theology: The Concise Sacramentum Mundi,* ed. Karl Rahner (New York: Crossroad Publishing Company, 1989), 1442.

28 Denis Edwards, *Ecology at the Heart of Faith: The Change of Heart that Leads to a New Way of Living on Earth* (Maryknoll, NY: Orbis Books, 2006), 76.

29 Ibid., 65–81.

30 Breviloqium, II, 12, 1. *Breviloqium: The Works of Bonaventure, Vol. II,* Translated from the Latin by J. de Vinck (Paterson, NJ: St. Anthony Guild Press, 1963).

31 Rahner, *Foundations of Christian Faith,* 190.

32 Ibid., 432.

33 For the Canadian Catholic Organization for Development and Peace's backgrounder on ecological justice, see http://www.devp. org/sites/www.devp.org/files/documents/materials/devpeace_back-grounder_2011-2016_ecological_justice.pdf.

34 John Paul II, "Peace with God the Creator, Peace with All of Creation," *World Day of Peace Message* (1990). No. 11 http://www.vatican.va/ holy_father/john_paul_ii/messages/peace/documents/hf_jp-ii_ mes_19891208_xxiii-world-day-for-peace-en.html (italics in original)

35 Canadian Conference of Catholic Bishops, *"You Love All That Exists ... All Things Are Yours, God, Lover of Life," A Pastoral Letter on the Christian Ecological Imperative, October 4* (2003). No. 17. http://www.cccb.ca/site/ Files/pastoralenvironment.html

36 Sister Marjorie Keenan RSHM, *From Stockholm to Johannesburg: An Historical Overview of the Concern of the Holy See for the Environment 1972–2002* (Vatican City: Pontifical Council for Justice and Peace, 2002).

37 Woodeene Koenig-Bricker, *Ten Commandments for the Environment: Pope Benedict XVI Speaks out for Creation and Justice* (Notre Dame, IN: Ave Maria Press, 2009).

38 Catholic Bishops' Conference of the Philippines, *What is Happening to our Beautiful Land: A Pastoral Letter on Ecology* (1988). http://www.cbcponline.net/documents/1980s/1988-ecology.html

39 Catholic Bishops of Queensland, *Let the Coastlands Be Glad: A Pastoral Letter on the Great Barrier Reef* (2004). http://www.catholicearthcare.org.au/pdf/ReefFullBooklet.pdf.

40 Bishop Luc Bouchard, *The Integrity of Creation and the Athabasca Oil Sands* (2009). http://www.dioceseofstpaul.ca/index.php?option=com_docman&task=cat_view&gid=15&lang=en

41 John Paul II, *Letter of His Holiness John Paul II to Reverend George V. Coyne, S.J. Director of The Vatican Observatory*. 1988. http://www.vatican.va/holy_father/john_paul_ii/letters/1988/documents/hf_jp-ii_let_19880601_padre-coyne_en.html

42 Max Oelschlaeger, *Caring for Creation: An Ecumenical Approach to the Environmental Crisis* (New Haven, CT: Yale University Press, 1994), 5.

Chapter 5

1 Pope John Paul II, *Letter of His Holiness John Paul II to Reverend George V. Coyne, S.J. Director of The Vatican Observatory*, 1988. http://www.vatican.va/holy_father/john_paul_ii/letters/1988/documents/hf_jp-ii_let_19880601_padre-coyne_en.html

2 Kenneth Miller "In Defense of Evolution." Nova, PBS. October 1, 2007. http://www.pbs.org/wgbh/nova/evolution/defense-evolution.html

3 Pope John Paul II Address to the Pontifical Academy of Sciences. Taken from *L'Osservatore Romano* Weekly Edition in English, 29 November 2000, page 5. http://www.ewtn.com/library/PAPALDOC/JP2ACSCI.HTM

4 Common Declaration on Environmental Ethics Common Declaration of John Paul II and The Ecumenical Patriarch His Holiness Bartholomew I. Monday, 10 June 2002. http://www.vatican.va/holy_father/john_paul_ii/speeches/2002/june/documents/hf_jp-ii_spe_20020610_venice-declaration_en.html

5   Charles Taylor, "Three Malaises." http://faculty.vassar.edu/brvannor/ Phil110/malaises.htm

6   Ibid.

7   Martin Luther King, Jr. Nobel Peace Prize acceptance speech, 1964. http://www.nobelprize.org/nobel_prizes/peace/laureates/1964/king-acceptance.html

8   Pope John Paul II, General Audience, 17 January 2001. http://www.vatican.va/holy_father/john_paul_ii/audiences/2001/documents/hf_jp-ii_aud_20010117_en.html

9   http://www.cccb.ca/site/Files/pastoralenvironment.html

10 http://www.cccb.ca/site/images/stories/pdf/enviro_eng.pdf

11 David Scott, "Spirituality," in *Christianity: The Complete Guide*, John Bowden, ed. (Toronto: Novalis, 2005), 1139.

12 Public lecture given by John Houghton at the University of St. Michael's College in Toronto, June 2002.

13 *The Christian Ecological Imperative*. Ottawa: Canadian Conference of Catholic Bishops, 4 October 2003.

14 The Jesuit Social Justice and Ecology Secretariat, *Healing a Broken World*, 2011. http://www.sjweb.info/documents/sjs/pjnew/PJ106ENG.pdf

15 Pope John Paul II, World Day of Peace Address, 1990. http://www.vatican.va/holy_father/john_paul_ii/messages/peace/documents/hf_jp-ii_mes_19891208_xxiii-world-day-for-peace_en.html

16 Pontifical Council for Justice and Peace, *Compendium of yhe Social Doctrine of the Church*. 2005. http://www.vatican.va/roman_curia/pontifical_councils/justpeace/documents/rc_pc_justpeace_doc_20060526_compendio-dott-soc_en.html

17 Pope Benedict XVI, *The Human Person, the Heart of Peace* (n. 8), 1 January 2007.

18 Bishop Luc Bouchard, "The Integrity of Creation and the Athabasca Oil Sands," January 25, 2009. http://www.dioceseofstpaul.ca/index.php?option=com_docman&task=doc_download&gid=14&Itemid=5&lang=en

19 Catholic Curriculum Cooperative Writing Partnership *Course Profile: Grade 9 Science (Open)* 1999.